Power Exchange Books'
Resource Series

ROPE, BONDAGE, AND POWER

Published by The Nazca Plains Corporation
Las Vegas, Nevada
2009

ISBN: 978-1-935509-02-8

Published by
The Nazca Plains Corporation ®
4640 Paradise Rd, Suite 141
Las Vegas NV 89109-8000

Cover Photo, Lochai
Art Director, Blake Stephens

ACKNOWLEDGEMENTS

Wow. Producing this book has been an emotional and physical whirlwind. First of all thank you so much to Dr. Robert Rubel (known as *Dr. Bob* at most conferences) for lovingly harassing me into taking this project on in the first place, then putting up with me as I coerced him to move the book from having six authors, to 12, to 17! You are an amazing spirit, and an amazing man — thank you for all your love and support.

This book could not have existed without my amazing authors — you were the team of writers I needed to help me break my anthology editing cherry. You hit deadlines (mostly ;)), you challenged my perceptions, you took criticism well, and you wrote some deeply touching and inspiring work — I look forward to the next projects you each have down the road — or just grabbing a drink some time.

Some authors were slated to be part of this book but had to back out for various reasons. Thank you DogTrainerUK, Miss Jaded and Scott Smith for the book ideas that then spurred on other authors — you just have to write for the sequel if Dr. Bob ever talks me into one! There were other amazingly supportive people within the Rope community who encouraged me to ask hard questions of myself and others — Jay Wiseman, Jimi Tatu, Ayem Willing, Boss Bondage... thank you all.

My kick ass copy editor, A. Scott Glancy, stepped in at last minute to polish this project with me until it glowed... thank you. To all of the people who had to put up with my authors writing late into the night on re-writes for me, or who had to re-read an essay for them 4 times, thank you for your patience. To my partners, friends, and people who expected emails to get read, thank you for your patience as well.

Lochai provided the beautiful cover imagery — thank you for helping me gift-wrap this present to the world. And for Nazca Plains, my publishers, I appreciate you delivering my baby and distributing it, and all of the hard work that goes into that process. However, this book would be nothing without you our readers. Thank you for demanding quality writing on sexuality, power, bondage, desire, passion, spirituality, and erotic authenticity. Thank you for going to classes, doing self-examination work, living passionate lives, and reaching out for more. Thank you for being sounding boards for our ideas... and arguing with us in return (or sending us love letters). You are a huge part of this process, and we could not do it without you.

Yours in Passion and Soul,

Lee Harrington, Editor
March 2009
Phoenix, Arizona, USA
www.PassionAndSoul.com

SERIES EDITOR'S PREFACE

Well, I'll certainly echo Lee Harrington's WOW! And then, I'll add a double WOW!! for Lee. What a tour de force. I've had a little experience coordinating around eight writers for issues either of Power Exchange Magazine or this Power Exchange Books' *Resource Series*, and even to **think** about coordinating seventeen writers sends chills down my back. Particularly, seventeen writers of the stature of these particular people.

This has been a fun read. One reason I love this volunteer job is that it gives me an ongoing stream of really pithy and interesting reading material. Another reason, is that I get to involve many of the friends I've met at conferences as contributors to these books. One of the funnier aspects of editing this series concerns names. My name, to be precise. There are three authors in this book who I believe do not associate my legal name with me. A couple of reasons. First, they don't know my last name, and in two cases, they know me as Corwin, my scene name from 2003 to 2006. I'm about to drop them notes on Fetlife (I'm Dr_Bob, if you'd like to exchange friends links).

Lee alluded to the growth of the number of authors from an initial six to an ultimate seventeen. There's a story, there.

Much of the fulfillment from being the series editor comes from my delight in being able to make such high-quality and interesting material available to our larger kink community. That, in turn, comes from having made some really interesting and competent friends during my kink travels. Each of the Issue Editors has brought their own personality to these books, and it's really interesting to see how much passion each pours into them. *Rope, Bondage, and Power* is one of the most passionately prepared books thus far in the series. When I finally contact the person who has asked to coordinate an issue, I present them with 6-8 people who have already told me of their interest (usually at a kink conference). Six to eight people are all that are needed to produce a 20,000-word 100-page book (the standard for our *Series*. Lee took one look at the list and asked whether he could expand it. "Sure," I said. The next thing I know, Lee emails me and asks how firm our 20,000-word limit was for the book. "What do you have in mind?" I asked. Well, Lee thought that he could produce a full-length book of about 40,000 words. It didn't take much arm-twisting after he told me who he had lined up for the project.

So, here you are. A full-sized book. When I sent it on to the publisher, and once he recovered from the shock that this was a 48,000-word full-sized book that he had not been expecting, he read it through. Within a few hours, he had called me back. "Wow," he said (at the risk of overusing "wow" in this brief preface) "This book is a major work, why didn't you tell me about it? This needs to be laid out differently than the other books in the series and promoted as a stand-alone book!" "Yep, works for me," I said. He had the entire book laid out and sent to me in about three hours. In the body of the transmitting email he asked, "How soon can you get this back to me?" I answered back, "By the end of the week." I could tell he was really impressed.

Now, for those of you who have been subscribers/purchasers of either the magazines or these resource books, I thank you not only for your ongoing patience as I struggle to get this material into print, but also for your tremendous support over the past two years. As always, if you also wish to be a contributor for any of these books, please contact me.

In Leather Heart and Spirit,

Bob Rubel (Dr. Bob)
PowerExchangeEditor@Yahoo.com

Power Exchange Books'
Resource Series

ROPE, BONDAGE, AND POWER

Issue Editor, Lee Harrington

Series Editor, Robert Rubel, PhD

TABLE OF CONTENTS

FORWARD:
ROPE, BONDAGE, AND POWER

by Lee Harrington

You stripped me
out of my defenses
and replaced each layer of armor with rough cord

Hands thrown back
you held me in my place
in my place in your arms [1]

I had been doing rope bondage in the public BDSM community for over 8 years when those words escaped onto the page and became part of the poem "With My Ankles in The Air." Five years later I can still remember the rope digging into my flesh, my world spinning, my partner laughing and me feeling their desire echo out with each line of hemp rope laid against my skin.

---

1 "With My Ankles In The Air" by Lee "Bridgett" Harrington first appeared in print in Raven Kaldera's anthology "Dark Moon Rising: Pagan BDSM and the Ordeal Path" from Asphodel Press, 2006.

Rope has power. Rope is a living thing. Unlike metal shackles, it can become more than a tool of restraint. It can be woven into body harnesses and corsets for decoration of the form. It can be braided into a whip to exact discipline onto waiting flesh. Rope can become a leash, a jump rope, a blindfold, a gag, a circle for creating sacred space.

This is what originally drew me to rope — its versatility. It can become so many things to so many people, and only the creativity and skill of the artist or rigger limits its potential for application. And it turns out I was not the only one who was drawn to this power of rope, and in turn how rope could be used to apply one's power or will to a partner.

When I first came into the greater world of kink exploration, taking tentative steps out of my bedroom games with my arms wide open to possibility, I had no idea there would ever be a Rope community. It was 1995 and in Seattle we were blessed to have the likes of Eddie who was looking at images coming over from Japan and trying to replicate them. Most of the other people in the space that we gathered would pull out leather restraints amazed at the guy who would take so long fooling around with line — don't you just want to get your lover tied up so you can get on to the good stuff?

But the truth is, for many of us, the rope is the good stuff. In the past 13 years, this fringe of the BDSM community has stood up and taken back the power of the B at the front of the well-known acronym. Bondage has come into its own right. Through events and gathering such as Austin Rope Symposium, ShibariCon, BodyBound, the Rope Dojo, Denver Bound, GRUE, and a fateful conversation at Black Rose one year, the Rope community in the United States has sprung into its own. We have realized we are not alone in finding rope to be an amazing tool to explore our passions, our fetishes, our desires... and yes, our power.

These evolutions within the North American Rope community were mirrored across the globe. In Japan, students of traditional Shibari and Kinbaku were opening their doors to outsiders wanting to study. In Germany, events like BoundCon sprang up not only to celebrate the erotic images of women in rope, but also to bring together in one place minds inspired by the potential of rope as a medium. In England and Australia the stages of fetish clubs provided a rich breeding ground for performance artists bringing rope to all new heights of creativity. This medium would eventually be picked up by mainstream performance groups such as Cirque du Soliel.

The message was and is clear — those of us exploring rope are not alone. And now the D/s (Dominant/submissive) community is taking note of the possibilities that rope has for them. Rope as ritual, rope as a way to build trust, rope as an expression of will... these things and more led to this book being born. When Dr. Ruebel asked me if I would like to coordinate the project, I knew that our community had too many perspectives to fit into a chapbook of essays. It was no easy trick to narrow down to just seventeen essays.

In this collection I have had the pleasure of bringing together authors living in Australia, England, Germany and the United States to speak about their various perspectives of how Rope, Bondage, and Power interrelate. I have a feeling that if I included another ten authors we would have ten more distinct takes on the subject. Yet again, rope bondage shows itself to be so amazingly versatile.

Graydancer, well known for his "Rope Podcast", examines the power or creating rope bondage rituals as well as when a piece of rope carries the power we have invested in it. Janice Stine in turn steps back and looks at the role of the rope itself as an active Dominant participant in play, as well as its role in submission in bondage play. Intention, technique, being in the moment and watchfulness are the key points for Zamil from Berlin, who examines how to seduce with rope.

For three authors, the idea of spirituality was of key importance when discussing the interplay of power and bondage. J.D. (half of the notorious Two Knotty Boys) looks at his own journey in "Zen Buddhism to explore the Way of the Zen Rope Master." Ariana Dawnhawk and Ryan team up to deliver an essay on bondage as it appears in history from Innana to Fenrir, Jesus Christ to Alistair Crowley. Mark Yu's take concerns the interplay between Ying, Yang and Qi in rope work, with some deep revelations within.

Maria Shadoes reminds us that the journey of power in bondage is deeply personal. She speaks about her childhood and overcoming performance anxiety. Madison Young opens up her bedroom and her soul with a deep look into feminism and submission, tackling the conflicting desires in our society. The issue of humanism, not just feminism, comes to a head with Coral Mallow speaking on the objectification of our rope models into canvases to be used to create our vision — not as lovers and friends.

It's not just women who enjoy being bound, as we see in the highly erotic tale of Van Darkholme, who talks about class issues and rope bondage in sexuality. Tony Buff and Mark da Silva also peer into the gay men's community and the experience of being a bondage aficionado in a world of leather.

For some of the authors, issues of definition and redefinition are key. Tonbi from Australia asks us to toss aside Top and Bottom, and instead look at the dynamics of the Giving and the Taking. LadyGold pushes us each to look at our own intentions and core needs both before and during negotiation with partners. Meanwhile, Klawdya Rothschild reminds us of the power involved in self-bondage, as we push ourselves to find power in our solitude — something often forgotten in a polarity-based community of desire.

LqqkOut poured himself into the issue using rope bondage as a language, and the power we gain as individuals when we learn how to use any language not just with competency, but fluency. Esinem, writing from London, took the concept of language to another level in the communication between bodies that occurs in the dance between people, reminding us our lovers are human, not parcels. Lastly Sarah Sloane opens a key concept: that bondage provides us with an amazing tool for catharsis and changing our lives, something often forgotten by those playing with bondage as simply a tool for getting it on (thought that is good too, so LadyGold reminds us).

Seventeen voices are not enough to encompass the entire Rope community. But these essays provide a microcosm of the macrocosm woven from our desires, accomplishments and potential. And in these amazing voices, rising over the sea of bickering (or worse, mediocrity), I am reminded of the greatness we can achieve as a cohesive Rope community. The power we can gain by working together, from a thousand varying perspectives, to build something great.

For those coming to this book having no idea what the Rope community is all about, or why rope is amazing, or what you can get out of rope bondage and power exchange — welcome to a feast for your senses! Inside these pages are both personal tales and analytical readings that will appeal to the engineers among you. You will find absurd silliness and profound magical moments. You will find courage, vulnerability, and creativity. But most of all you will find a chorus of power and rope that we hope you will some day add your own voice to.

Yours in Passion and Soul,

Lee Harrington, Editor
March 2009
Phoenix, Arizona, USA
www.PassionAndSoul.com

"CECI N'EST PAS UNE CORDE" THE PERSONAL SIGNIFICANCE OF ROPE

by Graydancer

"Shibari is communication between two like-minded people using rope...a connection between the hearts of two people. The rope should always embrace with love."

—*Akechi Denki (1940-2005), bakushi*

"[Magritte's work was] a juxtaposition of ordinary objects in an unusual context, giving new meanings to familiar things."

—*Wikipedia*

In his famous work, *The Treachery of Images,* Renée Magritte painted a typical tobacco pipe, something familiar to millions of people around the world. It was obviously a pipe, it could be mistaken for nothing else, it was a veritable Platonic ideal of a pipe. Then Magritte painted below the pipe *Ceci n'est pas une pipe* ("This is not a pipe") and blew people's minds. He was pointing out what was obvious but also often overlooked: it was not a pipe, it was a *painting* of a pipe. The fact that the human mind makes an association between paint on canvas and an actual pipe is simply a matter of assigning additional meaning to something that is, in itself, meaningless.

Sometimes a pipe is just a pipe, and sometimes it's just a word for something you can tie a pretty leg to (see, even the word *pipe* isn't a clear-cut thing). Before we start to talk about what rope means, let's get our terms straightened out.

Force is different than *dominance*. If I'm going to force someone to the floor, I do not need to be dominant — I simply need to take the steps necessary to get them there. Sweep the legs, twist the arm, pull the rug out from their feet, throw a banana peel in their path — that's force.

Dominance, however, is simply saying "Get on the floor." And for some reason, the submissive *does* it. Not because they're weak, but because they have the strength to surrender without losing themselves.

Dominance and submission are gifts, whereas force is simply applied physics. Rope can be both — like any fetish object, it can be assigned greater meaning than it inherently holds. Rope is just a tool, used to lift sails and control farm animals. It may also be used for the simple task of holding down a lover's limb — but then it may also become meaningful symbol of connection between you, a representation of that gift of dominance and submission.

The question becomes: how do we effect that change? When you come down to it, rope is just twisted fibers — produced in every country, in thousands of feet, and so ubiquitous that people hardly realize all the places they use it. This is supposed to somehow become *sanctified*? Yes. It does, and it can, both by choice and by circumstance.

It happens through the process of *significance* and *ritual*. It is a very personal process. Rather than try to provide a recipe, I present three examples of how rope has become a part of my own D/s path: gray, red and blue.

Gray

The gray rope is the simplest and most obvious example in my life of rope becoming D/s related. It was originally a gift from a play partner in Minneapolis who was experimenting with dying rope. She presented me with three lengths of cotton rope, each about fifteen feet long. It was a touching gift, as we no longer play much, a sort of token of appreciation for the part I'd once played in her life.

I used the ropes pretty indiscriminately for a few months. That changed in the summer of 2008 when I met and accompanied the model and rigger Sabrina Fox to Spankfestival, an outdoor camping event held twice a year in Black River Falls, WI.

Sabrina and I had started chatting on the internet long before the event, considering ourselves friends before we ever met face-to-face. When we met in person, that friendship became tinged with an intense attraction within a dominant-submissive dynamic. There wasn't negotiation, there wasn't a moment when she said "I submit to you." No, instead it was a simple as her laying her head in my lap as we watched a movie, and my hand resting against the side of her neck.

Something changed in that instant, and from that moment on, yes, we were friends, but there was no question about the dynamic. And we proceeded to explore that dynamic more and more thoroughly at the event and after.

At some point — a few days after the relationship shifted — I bound her wrists one morning in two of the three gray ropes. It's not a new technique for me — I find it quite handy to have rope shackles on a person even when not playing: they can be integrated into other ties, used as leads, etc. This time, though, I used the gray ropes, and that somehow lent a significance to the experience on a number of levels.

- These were personal ropes — not bought in bulk, presented to me as a gift.

- They were soft cotton — like a firm, warm caress around her wrists.

- The obvious point: they were the same color as my name, and so putting them on laid a kind of claim to her that was more clear than another color.

That last point, though it may seem trite, is actually more important in retrospect than one might think. Symbols have power — when she looked at that rope, it sent messages, *bound by gray.*

And it didn't only send messages to her. That rope, used during that couple of weeks we spent together, became indelibly associated with her. I have two lengths of it still — and I can't quite bring myself to use them on anyone else. They are the ropes I use *for Sabrina.* The third length I sent with her. It is more than a remembrance of a fun event — it is a memory of our connection, of that relationship between us. We do not have that relationship any more, though our friendship remains, but the ropes became imbued with those memories and associations.

Red

A couple of years ago I went through a life-changing event: the dissolution of my polyamorous relationship with my wife and my slave. Possibly the most difficult part of the breakup was the fact that I didn't have control over the events as things fell apart — and healing from it was a tremendously difficult.

One of the healing steps was the purchase of new rope — rope that had never bound my wife or my slave, rope that would represent a new start. This rope had been given an even greater meaning by the man who sold it, Twisted Monk, who had made a special color to support Midori's AIDS Life Cycle run. The layers of meaning touched me deeply:

- The rope supported AIDS research, a cause I am passionate about.

- The benefit was through the volunteer effort of Midori, a prime inspiration and teacher in my own development as a rope dominant.

- The color and conditioning of the rope was by Twisted Monk, a close friend who had helped me through the worst of the breakup.

- The rope would be the only set I owned that had not had the memory of those two partners of mine associated with it.

I decided that the rope itself should only be used on people that I was in a relationship with — not for demos or practice ties, this was going to be the Relationship Rope that represented my freedom from those painful memories.

There was an error inherent in my logic.

It was a year and a half later before I saw that error. It took a gift of some extra rope from a dear friend to make it clear. He had purchased some of the same batch from Twisted Monk that he'd used and had to cut, so it was an incomplete set. He is the kind of guy who dislikes incomplete sets, so he simply handed me half again as much rope as I had, the same high-quality hemp that I'd bought myself.

Suddenly that rope that I had imbued with the significance of "NOT-past relationship" became just another few ropes in my larger set. I began using in all sorts of situations, not based on what my connection was with my model, but based on what I wanted in my hands — based on my connection with *myself*.

I had come to realize that by making those ropes the representation of not being in those relationships, I was still giving power to my pain. By taking that symbolism away from the red ropes my own healing process was finally able to begin.

Blue

The blue rope has a bit more of a tale behind it. It's an unassuming thing — it is a ten-foot length of "Bridgett Blue" that I got in my very first rope sample kit from Twisted Monk. I used it often for tying hands as I began traveling more and more to events, and it was a well-used, well-loved rope.

At the Austin Ropecraft Symposium in 2007 I had the honor of giving the keynote speech, complete with good-natured heckling from Lee Harrington in the front row. Among the many respected names there at the symposium — a veritable Who's Anybody in Rope — Lee was one of the biggest, a force to be reckoned with.

And Lee liked me — we'd met and talked and even made out in the back row of some classes at Shibaricon. There hadn't really been any times to explore the attraction, until the Austin event, both due to circumstance and also my own experience. When Lee and I first met, I'd barely dipped my toe in the BDSM pool. In the years following I'd become a successful polyamorous Master and a performer, educator, and voice for the rope community. I'd gained enough self-confidence to accept an offer to play with him at that night's play party. In fact, I'd gained so much self-confidence that I accepted an offer to top both him *and* our friend Spike (a beautiful muscled trucker with a smooth head, a brilliant smile, and an amazing ability to give himself to pain and service) at the same time.

Yes, that's right. I was going to top two people at the same time, one of whom was one of the best-known names in the entire fetish/BDSM world. As I said, perhaps I had a bit too much confidence.

That certainly seemed to be the case at first, because I made a mess of things right from the start. I was nervous (*this is Lee fucking Harrington!*) and in public (*My god, Monk's over there, Madison Young over there, James Mogul, Lochai, Zamil, Mark of DV8, Jay Wiseman, holy shit, there's MAX! and MATISSE!*). Those actual words were not literally appearing in my head. No, it was manifesting in sloppy tying and unclear orders ("Kneel down, Spike!" "Yes sir!" "Wait, no, get me that carabiner!" "Yes sir!" "Oh, wait, I'm not ready for that yet...").

Spike, bless his soul, was in a zen-like state of simply taking what came to him. It's part of what makes him such an amazingly beautiful submissive, and I freely admit that I was squandering the gift he was giving me. Even worse, I was starting to absolutely irritate Lee.

There are, perhaps, submissives who can't tell when a top really doesn't have a plan, or when a dominant is uncertain. It is possible to hide the lack of purpose from these submissives, to keep them from realizing that you really are nervous, that you actually don't have much of a clue what to do *now* much less what you're going to do next.

Lee is not one of those submissives. Lee is an empathic switch with one foot constantly in the spirit world, as far as I can tell, and he could sense my nervousness. He tried getting me to relax. He tried telling me to breathe. Me, I tried rigging an upright suspension harness over the corset he was wearing and made a hash of it. I believe I tied a crotch rope, too, but that kind of hard to screw up, and boring, besides, without upwards tension. And every rope I put on just harshed Lee's submissive buzz more and more. At least that is how I saw it, and still do, years later.

I decided at one point that it would be a good idea to tie Lee's hands up to the suspension rope, which ran from his chest harness up to the hard point. Of course, this was higher than I could reach (especially with Lee's four-inch heels) and so I'd given Spike the uber-sexy order to "Get me a chair!" ("Yes sir!"). And standing on that wobbly chair, I was using the blue rope to tie Lee's wrists together over his head.

But I messed up the first time. So I unwrapped it and tried again. *Nope, too loose.* Try again. Nope, that seemed too tight — untie, begin again. Wait, maybe I should try that other tie I'd sort of learned in class that day...

At which point Lee screamed at me, there in the dungeon before God and everybody, "Goddamnit! Either tie my fucking hands or *don't*, but quit *dickin'* around!"

You could have heard a pin drop in the dungeon. It wasn't that big a space. That list of names I put up there? That's not an exaggeration; in fact, I left out a few. They were all there, they all heard Lee Harrington call me out on my ties.

At that point I had two options:

In option one, I throw down my ropes and storm out of the dungeon, maybe trying to feign anger but with the knowledge that I'd been humiliated in front of my peers. It wouldn't be too bad — as they say, it's no sin if you can't act Shakespeare — I'd bitten off a lot and Lee had violated the entire spirit of submission by disrespecting me in public. I would have been completely within my rights to leave.

But then I saw option two. It was not a clear path, but instead was a door inside my head that had cracked open, just a bit, and let me peek inside.

Inside Option Two was a scary world. It was a world of play that was a magnitude higher in intensity than I was used to. Instead of fleece-lined cuffs and soft leather floggers there was bloodstained leather and fist-sized bruises. There were few safe words behind that door, if any. It wasn't a happy sensual exploration of sex behind that — it was a forced march through the human psyche filled with cruelty and pain. It was the ordeal path, it was a dark and very scary place. It was a place I'd only read about. There was a large shadow in that place, shaped something like me, but darker, with a capacity for cruelty and sadism that I could only vaguely fathom, there at the doorstep.

I realized that if I went to Option Two, I would be saying goodbye to a comforting world of SM 101 and entering a darker realm of radical ecstasy. I realized, in that split second of humiliation and tension, that there would be no turning back.

I stepped through. I pulled that blue rope tight, tighter than I'd ever tied anyone, wrapped it around and around and didn't bother to lock it off or make a pretty little cinch, I just knotted the fucking thing and grinned savagely as Lee cried out at the sudden pain in his wrists. I smiled cruelly, because I knew it hurt, and because I heard the note of ecstasy in his moan.

I grabbed his throat. "You want to feel pain, you fucking slut?" I growled. "Pain is what I'll give you." I turned and started barking orders at Spike, while twisting nipples and slapping Lee's ass like I was trying to fell an oak. It was a passionate and dizzying scene after that decisive moment, with Lee-shaped ballet boot prints on Spike's back and my rope marks in a pattern of red left across Lee's flesh.

That blue rope, from then on, became a symbol: a symbol of my relationship with Lee (which has only grown stronger in the years since) and of my own growth and transition into a dominant. It became a symbol of that tipping point, when circumstances both forced me and provided the opportunity for cataclysmic growth.

Years later, I was privileged to help a young woman, MeganMarie, develop her kink. She'd found it like many do, playing around with her boyfriend, but when that relationship ended unpleasantly, she wanted to continue the kink without the complications. I was her rope buddy, and to this day some of the best work I've done was on her body. She graces the cover of my second book, and she has been one of the truest friends I've ever had.

At one point, I wanted to present her with something meaningful. I chose the blue rope, explaining to her the significance of it in my life. I told her that I saw her being transformed by her kink into something greater than she'd thought possible before. Humbly I asked her to accept custody of the rope as a symbol of that growth, just as it had symbolized Lee's catalyst within my own. She accepted, and it hangs from her bed, always in sight. She will either keep it or pass it on as she continues her own kink journey.

It is not a symbol of my dominance of Lee, or of Megan's submission to me. It is a symbol of submitting to our own journeys in BDSM, accepting the changes it demands of us regardless of the price. It symbolizes the trust we have that if we keep going through those doors, the person we are on the other side will be better than before.

It's a lot of meaning to give a ten-foot piece of hemp, because rope can be a tool, or it can become something more. It can become imbued with power, a fetish object it its own right.

It can bind us all together.

SEDUCED BY THE KISSES OF ROPE RITUALS AND MENTAL ENERGY

by Zamil

Intention

I want to map a path to expressions like "when you untie me, it feels like you undress me very tenderly" or "it was the most erotic encounter of my life".

This essay needs to go into the details of my emotional setup, the way I am and the way I do rope. It needs to cover lust and seduction; the aim to emotionally give and fill my partner; to be there, in the moment; to listen to and watch my partner very closely; to use the rope as an extension of my body, my touch and my emotions.

Levels of technique

Photos are great way to get an understanding about what's possible with rope. They are able to let me be part of the photographers world and understand the way he or she sees things. But Photos can't convey in a dynamic context of what has happened between the two persons involved during a session. It is a snapshot, a point in time.

Therefore, a photo doesn't tell me whether or not the rigger used the rope with utmost virtuosity, fumbled around, or anything in between the two extremes. It is like getting the final result of a football game on the news compared to being right there in the stadium, seeing it, watching the energy of the crowd, and being somehow connected with the team I fancy. An image is just the end result. Photos don't tell me anything about the rigger's abilities. They just show me (hopefully) good ties and that they know how to finalize a specific tie.

To my mind, there are at least two levels of technique when you do bondage. The first level is to know what to tie and the layout of a specific tie, e.g. a Takate-Kote. When we learn a new tie, we follow a certain pattern and the result will resemble, more or less, the layout we wanted to learn. But there is more to bondage than memorized ties. There is a second level. I like to compare it to playing an instrument and learning a new song. I need to know the melody, but just learning the new melody doesn't make this song alive, it will not have a soul. The interpretation, the soul, especially when doing classical music, is key to become a master. You need to integrate your soul into the music in order to make it more than just its melody and rhythm.

It is the same with bondage. Just knowing various ties and knots is not even half way down the road of learning. It is not so much a matter of "how to tie the tie." It is also a question of how the tie gets tied: how your soul finds its way through the tie into the session. The energy you tie with, which has its expression in the way the rope is applied, is different each day. But every time that energy is an intrinsic part of you and your soul. This energy is what an image can't show completely.

You can learn to be aware of your energy just as you can learn how to use it, but this is far more difficult to learn than just learning some new knots, bends or a new tie.

I think that far too much energy goes into understanding new ties and knots, and not enough goes into feeling the way we do rope. This is sad because the same tie applied with a different energy can be a complete new experience for both partners. Bondage technique, the way a certain tie is tied, is important for physically safety. A solid technique is the basis from which we start. There is no point going into the more emotional side of bondage while one is still contemplating when to go left or right, wrap or turn while applying a tie. We need to master the tie first before we can start experimenting with our energy.

When you do rope, there is a certain point at which all technique becomes part of you and you stop thinking about it. You just do it. The technique comes from within and flows through your hands into the rope. You don't need to think about it anymore, you just do it.

Once I reached this point other paths opened up; paths that are filled with the possibility to transform my inner lands into expressions in rope. Furthermore, my mind is now open to being right in the moment. The tie itself merges into the background as my partner is emerging from it. It is at this point that the way of the rope is guided by the energy of the moment, by my inner me and the setting which my partner and I are in.

Being in the moment

It is absolutely necessary that technique be no issue. While thinking about how to do something, you can't do it fully. Your mind is occupied, inner images and thoughts keeping you away from the moment. You may be there, but you are not fully *in* the moment. It took me years to completely understand and achieve this, and I truly learned it not through bondage, but through martial arts like Aikido. And even if "being fully in the moment" is understood intellectually, it is something completely different to make it part of your life; to live it — to get this knowledge from your brain down to your heart.

If my partner or myself are not solely in the moment, our experience, and the bondage itself, will not be as good as it could be. We have squandered the possibility of a wonderful adventure. To my mind, no human can be here and now all the time, but there are certain "tools" we can use to get us there. These tools I refer to as rituals.

Rituals

Rituals in this context are triggers or, in other words, a self-initiated conditioning used to set up and reach an emotional and cognitive state of mind and heart. Most of us have some type of rituals we use in various situations. Rituals are organized and systematized actions and can consist of things as diverse as mantras, breathing, symbols and more. I use rituals to prepare myself and to empty my mind. Rituals give me a defined set of actions to follow and while following each step my mind starts to relax, focuses on the actions I will perform and becomes serene.

"Setting the scene" is one of the rituals I use to open up to the upcoming play. This ritual contains all the necessary physical preparations, like getting the ropes out, setting up the ring if needed, checking my safety knife, getting some water, starting the music, fetching the toys and so on, but without having a special order. Setting the scene contains all actions necessary to fully prepare for a rope adventure. That frees my mind from all the details of my surrounding and the space I'm about to play in because I have set it up in a way that there is nothing more I need to get, regardless of what happens. I prepare as much as necessary in order to avoid leaving the scene, because something was forgotten. This frees my mind to be in the present.

Once the scene is set, I have done my best to get started and to be in ready mental-state. Breathe! It is important to me that my partner and I share the same noiseless freedom in our mind. This is not always possible right from the start for any number of reasons. We may not have done bondage together before; there may be blurry expectations, projections; or sometimes a feeling of insecurity or nervousness might prevent us from reaching that ready mental-state. It is obvious if I'm insecure within myself and my partner will sense it. What is true for feeling insecure is true as well or feeling secure, and any other feeling I may have. My partner will feel whatever I am projecting.

If you have been into rope for a while, you may have had the experience that the same tie, for example a Tasuki, can be applied differently. It is a different experience if you unroll your rope first, then forcefully grab the wrists of your partner, force them onto the back, and start tying. Or perhaps you wrap your arms around her, kiss her gently on the side of her neck and unroll the rope in front of her. Let her skin feel the gentle touch of the short end of your rope from throat to navel while moving your hands slowly down to her wrists. Different starts lead to different energy that gets into the scene right from the beginning. The rituals involved here are paving the way into and mindset of the scene.

Another good start for me is the Reiki-Start. Reiki is a form of energy that floats through us all the time and can be channeled for various, and only positive, purposes. I use that sometimes if the partner I'm tying is unknown to me and... interesting. The purpose of this start is to build a relaxed and calm inner environment in my partner, paving a road for all unnecessary fears and blockages to move on, opening up the soul for the experience to come, focusing on the here and now, and building up trust. Any short focused sexual energy will be diluted and the vibes between us will be just right to connect.

Watchfulness

Watchfulness to me is key during a session. It includes monitoring my partner to see whether or not everything is still OK and how she feels and reacts. What is usually understood is that any medical issue arising needs immediate attention. That may be a compressed nerve or constricted blood circulation. But the issues that throw my partner or I out of a good scene in no time are rarely medical in nature.

One of those issues is when the end of the rope hits my partner in the face or neck. What I see often is that riggers tend to learn a tie but completely ignore their partner when they tie. The rope is an extension of myself, it doesn't lie and will behave exactly the way I guide it. Anything I do to the rope will be a message to my partner. Regardless of how experienced with rope my partner is, she will read that message and translate it. This is also true for anything I don't do. All my actions, and even inactions, will be a message to her. I don't think that any of us likes being seen as a careless bully or not taking our partner's well-being into account. To me it is absolutely necessary to be in control of the rope at its full length. That means that I know where all of my current rope is and how it will behave if I'm tying this wrap or that turn in slow motion or at speed.

Rope can behave like a whip sometimes. It can just whip around an angle or turn and ends up somewhere. Hitting my partner unintentionally with my rope is something I really have to avoid, regardless of what the final result looks like. It goes without saying that unintentionally scratching my partner with my nails or getting the rope tangled in her hair falls into the same category of things to prevent. What it needs is the complete control of my movements and the rope at its full length at all stages to prevent that.

But this is only one part of what I call watchfulness. There are always more things to take care of and actions to control. For Example, it is impossible for my partner to get her hair out of her own face while in rope, and that can tickle. It is my responsibility to take care of the major issues, like making sure she still feels OK and that no nerves are compressed, but also to consider even those minor issues that may interfere with a perfect experience in rope.

And again, in order to fully control my movements, the rope, and to monitor my partner all at the same time I need to be fully in the moment.

Emotional Setup

Bondage to me is a way to express myself and my myriad emotions. All of us can have an awful lot of emotions regardless of whether we can put a name to them, or even whether we are able to express them. This is certainly true for me. It is also true that being equipped with various options to express emotions helps anyone to survive life better. A whole industry has been developed around exploring these options.

My emotions vary from day to day but the general direction — my emotional setup — remains the same. My emotional setup is the general outline of my emotions and my ability or non-ability to express them. This basic layout of my inner self, my inner land, is visible all over my bondages and the way I do rope. To my mind, there is nothing much I can do to change that; it is me.

All my emotions have a certain energy they come connected with. In my inner land, anger, for example, comes connected with a powerful, destructive, outside facing, hot energy like a volcano. Love comes like a constant flow of warm, orange water. And lust as a multicolored firework, sometimes quiet and sometimes it explodes. These are my translations of some of my emotions into inner images or areas of my inner landscape. You may have or create different images, but whatever images you choose, they are all expressions of yourself, your soul. As your emotions have developed, so have these images formed inside of you too, and now they are an intrinsic part of yourself.

Those images and emotions can be expressed in bondage much the same way that an artist who uses paint to to express their emotions when they create on a canvas.

The tie I choose to start with is an expression in itself because it determines certain aspects of the session. Tying someone spread-eagle is generally different from applying a Hojo-Jutsu techniques. Another way to express those inner images is the relative strictness and tightness of a tie. A powerful tie will become tighter than a sensual flowing one. All that is clearly visible even when the tie is final. But there is more to it.

During a takedown scene I apply rope differently than I do while having a slow and warm session with my partner. The energy of both settings is different and the ties will be too. But to me, both settings are rather simple in their energy because the energy doesn't change, but stays the same. It is like painting an image just with one color. That can be absolutely stunning, but it will still be just one color.

To change energy while applying rope is very different and a little bit more difficult. Instead of thinking in whole ties, I separate a tie into its components – wraps, turns, layers or fixations – and for each component I seek to have many different to do them in order to express what I feel, or what I want to make my partner feel. Each component can now be connected with a different energy and therefore the whole tie, and the session, will have more variety and depth.

This emotional setup and its expression in rope is nothing one could prevent. It is always there and it is just a question of how it finds its way into the rope. It is just a question of whether you are using it intentionally or unknowingly.

Wrap up

All the energy I've been speaking about so far has been my own. But this is a very limited perspective because there is still my partner and his or her own emotional setup and energy. When it comes down to it, and all curtains have been raised, bondage means to open up fully to yourself and your partner. This is what makes it so special and even more intense than having sex. If I open myself up fully, I just can't think about technique anymore. It just needs to float. This gives me the possibility to be in the moment, alert and watchful sensing current needs, my emotions, and the emotions of my partner, to set up and guide us through the scene we are in. It gives me the choice to either take her with me into my emotional land or to adjust my actions to melt into hers.

One could argue that in order to really become a master of this expressionistic way of rope, one has to learn all the things I was talking about. But even if someone has learned all that, chances are that it will not be what was intended. In my own experience, learning all this was just one step forward, while the next step is to forget it all again and just live it. Fully, and in the moment.

EXCHANGING POWER WITH THE ROPE

by Janice Stine

Rope bondage is a very special type of play. Unlike impact or many other types of play, rope plays a unique and consistently active role as a form of bondage. Where in impact play, the implement is used to strike and is then withdrawn; rope maintains contact with the person being bound. This creates a power play between the dominant and the rope, as well as between the submissive and the rope. The rope interacts submissively toward the dominant while, at the same time, being dominant to the submissive. As a result of this, I believe that there is an important power dynamic not only between the people involved in a rope scene, but also between each person and the rope itself.

In many ways, rope acts as submissive to the dominant. Just like I do not necessarily want to play with every submissive I see, I do not want to use every piece of rope that I pick up. I choose my rope based on how it lays on the body, what kind of texture it has, and my general idea of the direction in which I would like the scene to go. These are the factors that are very important to me.

As I talk with a potential submissive partner, I start to form an idea in my head of what kind of scene it could be. I listen to the way in which they describe what they like, looking for key concepts that will allow me to create an experience in which they will come away feeling fulfilled.

If they tell me that they enjoy rough sensations and fighting against the rope, for example, I would choose a rougher fiber that will make their escape from the rope that much more uncomfortable. Usually, this will be a new or almost new piece of rope; one that I have not worked with as much, and am less familiar with. This rope will be less worn and have little or no experience with my intentions. It will not lay around the body as smoothly, and have an inherent stiffness that has yet to be broken down. This rope will likely be just as firm and challenging to wrangle as the bottom I am playing with. As this rope is used, it will become softer and more flexible, eventually becoming the rope that I would use in a situation where the submissive is not a fighter, finding new rope to replace it, and replacing older rope with it as it loses its strength and integrity.

Alternately, if I were negotiating with someone who told me that they want to play with rope because it feels like a hug, I would likely choose soft, comfortable rope that will enhance that sensation. Often that involves finding a piece of rope that I use often, that has become soft and more pliable due to the regular use and conditioning. This rope is well used and well loved; a projection of the feelings that I am passing through it to the submissive I am playing with. In this way, I am passing my dominance through the rope and onto the submissive.

My rope becomes submissive to me immediately upon pulling it out of the toy-bag. The way I remove it and my intention behind it set the tone for the scene. The rope uncoils as I remove whatever knots I used to put it away. I like to use ropes that I have put away using knots which will pop open quickly and easily so that I can move quickly into the scene without having to fumble with the rope. In this way, I am able to immediately exert power over it, uncoiling it and running my hands over it to make sure that it is viable for the scene, and finding the center point to create a bight, which I can use as a starting point to bring my vision to life.

The rope follows my direction, wrapping around the body of whomever I am tying, using its own friction to hold itself in place. It lies wherever I place it, creating a binding that follows my intention. If the placement of the rope is not what I want, or the person I am tying is not reacting in a way that is working for both of us, I can easily move it somewhere more suited to the progression of the scene. Once it is on the body, it does not move, other than slight shifts as the submissive moves in it. It waits for me to decide what to do next. When I am ready for it to come off, it does. If I want to use it in a different way or lay it in another configuration, it complies. I can easily take someone from one position to another, adjusting the bindings to fit any position I can think of. Rope is very adaptable in that way.

The rope will adjust in many ways to suit my needs. I can use it to bind someone or to create some other type of implement. I can leave it in a coil and use it for impact play, or braid it and use it as a dildo. It can be tied into the shape of a strap-on harness, used as a flogger, a blindfold, or a gag. I especially enjoy mixing different possibilities together, using the rope as a tool for bondage and for impact play in the same scene, for example. I have had wonderful scenes where the only toy I had with me was rope, and I was able to bind someone and do impact play with them in ways that they did not expect. It can be used on almost any part of the body for a multitude of purposes. It is versatile and very capable of serving in the many ways that I might desire. The only limit to how the rope will serve is my imagination.

There are occasions where the rope does not act as obediently as I would prefer. Rope will sometimes knot itself, like a willful submissive finding a way to take the scene in another direction. However, I am able to untie the knots, guiding the rope in the direction I have chosen, or adjusting it so that the knot it made in itself has no impact on the scene itself. As with any submissive, I administer discipline and there are consequences to misbehavior. If the rope refuses to let go of knots of its own making, I toss it to the side and use another piece. If the rope is beginning to unravel or otherwise shows weakening in its structure, I will put that piece to the side, or cut off a viable section to make it more immediately useful.

I maintain my ropes and care for them as my property, showing them the proper attention both before and after a scene. Before the scene, I will run my hands over them, making sure that they are clean and that there was no damage sustained by them previously that I did not notice. I coil them after play, clean them, and check them for frayed ends and weak areas that need to be removed. In return, the rope maintains its inherent submission to my ideas for its use.

Rope also has a quiet, assertive dominance toward a submissive. There is an interesting paradigm in that the rope can, at the same time, be submissive to the dominant and dominant to the submissive. The power of the rope is so intense that, in some cases, endorphins and subspace begin before the rope is even put on the submissive. I start to go into a calm, happy space within moments of being in contact with rope that will be binding me. When I am being bound, the aroma of certain kinds of rope can begin to transport me before a piece even touches my skin. There is one type of rope in particular that I do not even have to see, just the smell of it is enough to evoke a certain level of endorphins, whether there is the potential that I will be playing with it or not.

In rope bondage, there is a duality of interaction. A submissive is not only interacting with a dominant person, but also with the dominant force of the rope. Once the rope has been placed on the body, a submissive will begin in some way to interact with it. In this interaction, there are many variations, depending on the submissive's personality and mood, as well as the inherent energy of the scene. Sometimes he or she will curl up within the rope, enjoying the inherent strength of the fibers. Others will test the rope, pressing their bodies against it in order to confirm that they are actually bound, and that it will not fall away. Then there are those who will fight the ropes, manipulating them and working their way out of the binding. Many times, the rope will win, and the submissive that is fighting will not be able to get out. There will be times where the submissive is able to escape, giving him or her great satisfaction at having accomplished their goal. In each of these cases, the rope pushes back, asserting its strength. The rope does not give way without a fight. In this situation, rope that breaks or too easily gives way can lose power in a scene just as easily as a dominant reacting in this manner would. The submissive's attention is divided between the person initiating the action and the constant contact with the rope against their body.

Sometimes the rope is the entire scene. The submissive is tied and allowed to savor the feeling of being in bondage. In these cases, the rope takes on an increasingly more dominant role. When I have been placed into this kind of bondage, everything else goes away. I am dominated by the constriction of the rope, the positions that it is holding me into, the awareness of everything that is even slightly uncomfortable. The submissive then turns inward, curling up into the rope, shows an inherent knowledge that the rope has control over them. When I go into this space, I have given up control to the rope. I am not fighting to get it back, but being accepting of the rope, as well as the desire of the person who put me into the bondage. This type of situation creates a space where the dominant need not be actively engaged to show their dominance, as they have delegated that responsibility to the rope itself.

When watching a submissive struggle to get out of the rope, the intense, if subtle dominance of the rope is obvious. There is no person keeping them in the rope. Often, the person who did the binding is not actively participating during this part of a scene, but is watching as the submissive struggles. I get a great amount of satisfaction being able to watch a submissive fight against a tie that I have done. I know that with enough skill and determination, the submissive may be able to get out, but that the rope is not going to make it easy for them, either by letting go or by falling away. Knots generally do not undo themselves. At some point, either the dominant decides to remove the rope, or the submissive manipulates his or her way out. At this point, the scene can either move in another direction or come to an end. When the scene is over, the power exchange with the rope starts to fade. The ropes are taken off, cleaned, coiled back into their original bind, and put away. Much like kissing a dominant's boots after a scene, coiling rope that has been used on me brings a sense of contentment and closure.

The rope once again is neatly put away, showing its possession by the dominant, and the care and reverence of it by the submissive. It is put back into the place where it will wait until the next opportunity presents itself. It has had one more experience that will show in its next use, becoming more pliable and conditioned in a way to better suit the dominant's needs in future uses, while maintaining its innate strength and unique features making it perfect for keeping control of the submissive the next time.

ON THE OUTSIDE LOOKING IN WITH A FIST FULL OF ROPE

by Van Darkholme

In the carnival of life, my genetic coin toss started off very promising. It landed solidly on a silver platter, bounced off onto another, but equally opulent, platter. Then, unfortunately, it slowly rolled off into the dark crevices.

To put it mildly, we weren't middle class. Visions of the entire family loaded up in our old Buick station wagon for a 45-minute ride to McDonalds, Merle Haggard was blasting on the radio as I was watching Route 66 dashing by through the rusty holes of the Buick floor, and my stepfather's unfiltered Camel cigarette smoke beat against the wind but never quite escaped the vehicle... never quite escaped me to this day.

It's funny that a small isolated town surrounded by cornfields was so obsessed with class.

School was hell. I was trying to fit in but it was hard without the right clothes, the right car, and the right house. The ones labeled with Izods and Calvin Kleins stuck together, Fruit of the Looms and Wranglers were scattered about in their own individual self-loathing hell. Johnny was a handsome football player, and his father was the town banker. His coin landed squarely on the glistening gold plate. He was always smiling, driving through town in his red vintage Mustang convertible. It was so cliché but it's true: his girlfriend was a beautiful blond cheerleader, Debbie. I think their coins landed on the same plate.

The cruel gods went even further by injecting me with a massive amount of testosterone in my teens, and the results were acne and erections. I even got acne on my erection... but that didn't stop me from doing something about it. An unexpected mirage appeared through my cracked windshield. I caught a glimpse of Johnny's Mustang dancing in the heat on the side of a quiet country road. The hood was open and all I could see was his ass in tight blue jeans.

I pulled up in my old man's truck. "Need some help, Johnny?"

Even in hot, bucolic surroundings, Johnny always seemed as if he was just freshly showered and there was never a wrinkle on his clothes. He turned around and seemed disappointed to see me.

"Naw, it's just a fan belt, " he said. Then he dove back under the hood of his car. My desire for him was like a distant train. Without any warning, it came barreling right at me fast and loud. My heart was about to jump out of my chest as I grabbed a coil of cotton clothesline on the truck seat and headed straight for him. Sure, sports gave him a fantastic physique and plenty of strength — but it's nowhere compared to my years of working on the farm and wrangling beasts of burden. I dragged him to the middle of the cornfield and made a nice clearing with my muddy boots. His torso was bound tight but I managed to rip off the top of his shirt to expose his hard pecs. I shoved the fabric deep into his mouth. His eyes jabbed at me with fear and anger so I pulled out a wad of hankie from my Wranglers and made his world black. He thrashed his legs about like an animal. I punched him a couple of times to settle him down.

Off came Johnny's the designer jeans. They felt nice and warm. I was puzzled... besides the label, his jeans didn't look anymore different than mine and yet it made all the difference at school. I decided I'd better tie his ankles. I sat on a pile of jagged corn leaves and watched his partially naked body. I told myself to remember every inch of his body: his golden brown hair, the sculpted ridge of his nose, his pale pink nipples punctuating his meaty pecs, the dark curly patch of hair just right above the band of his tightie whiteys, the thick muscular striation down his thigh, and his perfectly manicured toes. Time passed. His breathing and mine subsided. For some reason, I looked around to be sure that we were really alone. I slowly reached out and brushed my hand against his crotch. His face turned toward the ground and he made a soft moan. His huge cock pushed out against the white cotton fabric. For the first time in my life, I came face to face with everything I dreamt of and everything that I was not. And, it responded.

It would have been stupid for me to think that Johnny and I would ever have any sort of sexual interaction. The material for my masturbation fantasy was more credible if I took him against his will. I visited that dusty road mornings, nights and every chance I got. I saw him at school and he had no idea...He kept on smiling and continued with his charmed life.

I left town the day following my high school graduation. I did not waste any time. Perhaps there was hope in the big cities like Los Angeles. After several menial jobs, I was dismayed to find that LA was just a mega-version of my hometown. I was so young and so naive. One hot and smoggy afternoon, I took refuge in a small bookstore. I saw a painting of a man in rope bondage by Goh Mishima and something very familiar struck me deep down to my core. I was amazed that bondage was presented as art. There were some weird electrical connections in my brain and I grew on to associate bondage with money. At that moment, I decided to tie up men as a part time job.

Soon, I was a busboy by day and by night I was in total control of some Hollywood executive. It wasn't long before I quit my day job. For the first time in my life, power was handed to me on a plate and I loved it.

"Hi Steve, how are you? Please come in." I smiled to a nervous stranger at my door. "Go in my bedroom, take off your clothes and wait."

In my darkened bedroom, Steve had a raging hard-on even before I laid my hands on him. I tied him up tightly and secured him to my bedposts. Again, I preferred my subject blindfolded. A mélange of power, adrenaline and sexual impulses came over me. He was processing powerlessness and fear into carnal energy. I whispered into his ear, "I got you all tied up and I'm going to play with you all night long." Steve whimpered, "Yes, Sir. I'm all yours." I punched his chest and tugged hard on his balls, "What makes you think I want you?" He cried out in pain, "Oh God, I'm sorry Sir. That was presumptuous of me."

Steve was experiencing sex in its purest form. The rope pressing down on his flesh constantly reminded him of his body and its physical sensation. His vision was impaired and his other senses kicked in. Being bound, nothing was required of him.

No thinking about the next sexual move. No gauging the other partner for any sort of physical or emotional connection. No time to be self-conscious about his body or his being because he was reduced to a powerless bound object. Steve's humanity was pushed aside for a moment: just enough time for him to feel the sensation on his cock and in his mouth and perhaps other parts of his body, without any other distractions. In the self-absorbed culture of Los Angeles, the only kinky taboo left for Steve was to offer himself completely to someone like me on the fringe of society. Yet, afterwards, he jumped into his shiny Lexus and safely returned to his home... to his life.

"Hi Dave, how are you? Long time no see. Please come in." I looked at a young handsome man in a business suit. "Hi Van, I tried to call you several times when I was in town but no luck." We both walked into my bedroom. "I'm sorry, I was in Paris for a month." Dave knew where to hang his clothes as I offered him a beverage. After a quick formality, he reached out and hugged me. "Gosh, I missed you so much, Van." After four years, I was still taken aback when I received the same warm greeting from Dave. He liked to get tied up with hemp ropes. He loved the smell of leather. He liked to give up control and be totally helpless. He enjoyed receiving oral sex but nothing further than that. I enjoyed watching him as I stroked and teased him. He begged. He pleaded. He cursed. His arms tugged hard against the tight ropes as he let out a raw primal scream. He exploded.

As always, he quickly jumped in the shower and then put himself back together as we made small talk. I picked up the towels, "How's your wife and kids?" He brushed his hair, "Oh, they are great. We just took the little one to Disneyland for the first time. Hey, I'll be back in July. Will you be in town?" I was walking him to the door, "Gee, so far I have no plans, so I should be here." He reached out and kissed me. Dave seamlessly vanished into the muggy Los Angeles rush hour.

It was quite ironic. I spent my teen years masturbating to fantasies of tying up Johnny and in my adult life the Johnnys of the world came to me to get tied up. I knew why I had the desire to tie them up: to temporarily possess things I wanted but never had. When I looked at these men tied up in front of me, it was more than a body. It was a product of regular dental visits, a full college education, Norman Rockwell Christmases, and a nurturing family life. My ropes became symbolic ribbons presenting me with these gifts for an instant in time. In spite of all the elements of a privileged life, Johnnys visited the likes of me in the seedy, dark gay ghetto. They engaged in debauchery — but in a way, it was against their will because they were powerless in bondage. My powerful hemp ropes glowed with the dim ember of societal constraint.

There are many different dynamics in bondage. The above reflects a portion of my bondage play. I was young and I needed the money...(smile), I wouldn't change a thing. The insights, knowledge and practice I got from this early period have served me well. I realize that we all couldn't fit on the gold plate and I'm fine with that. I used what I had in the best way that I knew how. Being on the outside looking in sometimes has it's advantages.

SURRENDERING TO THE VISION

by Coral Mallow

I hold a length of hemp coiled to my liking resting patiently in one hand. In front of me waiting eagerly, are willing assistants. Neither of them gives me input beyond their physical limitations and assets. This is not about beautiful rope or sexy spiritual people. This is about the creation of integrated time based art. They are supplies, untapped potential, and the media for my art. They are pieces of the whole, like the space we occupy, the sounds they will create, the light playing across their skin, and the amount of endurance they have either emotionally or physically for this moment. They have surrendered themselves to being useful objects so that I may in turn surrender to my muse. In the case of rope bondage as art, the power exchange involves individuals submitting not just to the dominant, but to the Creative Process and the Vision.

I have run into many people who believe that rope bondage, while artistic, is not art. I find this logic to be, at best, faulty. Necessity led to the development of rope being used in many ways from farm work to warfare. Human imagination and creativity led to the development of these uses into highly stylized forms such as macramé, sailing knots, and hojojutsu. From these and other disciplines we as kinky people embrace, alter, enhance and use them for BDSM. If we define art as the products of human creativity than we can easily make the leap of rope bondage being a form of art. The artistic vision and drive can be born from the top, the bottom, joint conceptualization, or a third party. It can be a solo venture. The art can be the basis for other styles of creative endeavor such as theatrical performance or photography. The art can be the process of tying and untying, creating a constantly changing vista rather than a static end result. Like the extensive variety of our play it can be passive or aggressive, stand alone or interactive, rope only or other media inclusive, silent or boisterous, soul ripping catharsis or silly fun time, but the dominant overriding factor is the urge to create a visual, textural, and temporal piece of art.

When I was finding my voice in rope work, I had not made this correlation. I was studiously practicing my ties and knots, garbling Japanese terms in an attempt to show that I had read all the pertinent books. Anyone who was willing to teach, I was willing to watch and learn from. I had such love for the act of tying someone up, down, to whatever and whomever that it never occurred to me to look for a deeper purpose other than it was great fun. Power dynamics only entered into play with the partners that enjoyed it or needed it. At the time my concept of power dynamic was heavy D/s interplay that began and ended with the scene, or it was the exact opposite with me smacking them on the butt, looking them in the eye with a big smile and a heartfelt "Quit wiggling! I'm tying over here!" Part of the reason for this approach was the very relaxed community that I came up in. Part of it is the type of Top that I am. Yet the largest piece was, when it was all new, that my purpose was to learn, to stretch myself, and try out ideas. To transport my partners through physical sensation was all that I knew.

A day finally came when it transformed into something more. When I walked up to a play partner of mine stating that I wasn't interested in them I just needed a canvas. She saw it as objectification and was delighted. I didn't particularly care how she felt to be completely honest. I had an idea. My idea, my thought and I had to see it realized. I didn't feel the rope in my hands as I normally do. I do not remember smelling it. I could only interact with it as I shaped it to my partner's form and the tie points. My focus was heady and acute. I tied and tied until I got stuck on one point that wasn't lying just right. I proceeded to work on that one detail for almost as much time as it took to tie the rest of it until it was perfect. Then I stood back and looked. I wasn't looking at her or the rope work I had done. I was looking at my creation, a piece of art that had sprung from that deep place in me that sculpts and paints, sings and dances. I ran my hands over the three dimensions of flesh and rope, light and sound and then, I destroyed it. I went back piece-by-piece and undid every knot and hitch. The deconstruction of my work was every bit as sensation heavy to me as its creation. When I handed her to her aftercare I let myself hold the uncoiled rope, my shattered pottery, my torn canvas. The remains of my art in my arms not gone but waiting to be gathered up to become another Vision at another time. I had given in to the impulse so completely that it dominated my mind and senses driving me to better myself. I was the Top and I was not in topspace. I was in subspace. I was elated.

A couple of years later I came to be in the possession of something rather odd for me, a piece of Human Property who is not a rope bottom. This was a piece of trouble emotionally for me when I wanted to throw rope. He would dutifully stand for me, but shared no energy back. My difficult bondage and perfectly executed ties were of no interest to him. I received no satisfaction of doing what I enjoyed as my Boy just took it to make me happy. The power exchange was anemic at best. So I focused on other types of play and shoved this piece of myself aside for that relationship. Then I was asked to help another partner do some rope for photography on his bondage website. When we met up the plan was that I would do the ties and my Boy would take the photos. He and I tossed ideas around, came up with a few scenarios and away we went! The moment came on the third scenario when I switched mental space from tying him up for pictures and began to create art. He donned a Zentai encasement suit covered in written poetry and I slipped into that focused delirium as the rope danced, the positions changed, and together we made art. It was especially brilliant to be tying with someone who could and did let go of self to become not just my layer, but his layer of art as well. We were both very drunk on the experience and smiles bounced happily over the uncoiled rope afterwards. The Boy taking pictures the entire time had a blast behind the camera and mentioned nothing to me of what he thought of it all.

Several days later my Boy comes to me with a new light in his eyes. He formally asks to speak with me. We sit down and I ask what he wished to speak about. He replied that he wanted to be my Art. That's where he could go with the rope work. He had no interest in the medium for play as either a top or a bottom but craved feeling that energy from me, to loose himself in my creativity and be transformed through my play. He couldn't submit to the rope, not being able to see it as anything but a tool, and he had already surrendered himself to me. To give up who he was for my creative vision was challenging and intoxicating to him. So we began working down that path enhancing our D/S relationship to our mutual (so far) satisfaction. His interest in becoming art was so exciting to him that we wound up taking an Art History class at the local community college. He garnered a new appreciation of art in general and I found some new nifty ideas! I will admit that it was a turn I never thought would happen out of BDSM play.

There are many reasons that appeal to people who choose to be art supplies, the biggest of which is that they get to be a piece of Art. Not just any art: Your Art. That they, for a moment in time, will be a unique vision that will never be seen again even if you tie them the exact same way at another time. It is ambrosia to them. My male partners tend to enjoy the end result more than the process, while my female partners tend to be the opposite. I am always amazed at the emotional and spiritual release especially from my bearish and full-bodied assistants, when the societal norms slide away and they can be perceived as beautiful without being diminished by a size bias. On the other end of the spectrum, my thinner bottoms tend to like being transformed into something powerful and grotesque. That does not mean I will not use a larger person for shocking or disturbing purpose, nor do I shirk from using a lean body to state more classical beauty. It has simply been the feedback of my human tools from my artistic journey. Your experience will differ from mine as drastically as sculptures differ in a gallery.

The layers of surrender for the bottoming side are many and include (but not be limited to): separation from self, surrender knowing that the top is competent, art enhancing either your best or worst qualities, and being challenged by what you perceive as sexual and sensual. There is the surrender that though you become art, it may not be art you appreciate or even like. There is the surrender of the time it takes to be tied not just to completion, but to satisfaction. I have had bottoms, who could not stand to be bound, wait and hold themselves in check so I could complete my vision. The idea that it was for art kept them from their usual reaction of screaming and pulling it off them. They allowed the art to be completed then literally one second later demanded its removal, which they waited patiently for me to do. Being an art supply helped in facing that bottom's fears around being bound if only for the space of the act. I myself have been able to push past pain and discomfort for the sake of allowing an artistic vision to be realized. I admit to being shocked at having more endurance for art than for even my own bottoming needs.

My path as a rope artist has been at times frustrating as well as fulfilling. I have ended "projects" when they would not work. I have agonized over location and lighting, at times choosing not to play when they would not work for my needs. I have undergone the requisite feelings of being inadequate to the other artists that have come before me and sometimes even right next to me in a dungeon. Some of my art has been carefully planned and constructed. Some has happened by complete accident. I have rejoiced in bondage styles from minimalist to traditional, from militaristic to jazz. I have quite happily delved into many types of multimedia. I continue to surrender myself to my creativity, to my ideas and ideals of what should and could be. I allow for growth not just as a rope Top, but as an artist as well. Whether done to you or another, many participants or a select one, the power exchanged to create and actualize the Vision leaves a powerful and lasting impression, even as the only proof of its existence fades with our bruises and rope bites.

THE GIVING AND TAKING OF ROPE

by Tonbi

There are two sides to rope bondage, The Giving and The Taking. Now I'm not talking about the bottom giving up control and the Top then taking the control that is offered. I'm talking about The Giving, or non-resistance, is where the bottom offers or gives themselves to the Top. They actively, or passively, assist the Top as they are being tied up. The Taking, or resistance, is where the bottom fights against being tied up to some level. Now just to be clear, in both situations it is the bottom's final goal to be tied up, and the Top's objective to tie the bottom up. However, there are different paths available to get there and sometimes those paths cross or run parallel to one another.

Let's look at examples of each path:

The Giving (non resistance)

Her eyes passed slowly over the neat coils of rope that lay in front of her kneeling form as she patiently waited for him to enter the room. The sound of his steps announced him mere moments before he appeared in the doorway. He surveyed the room with a casual glance and then smiled at her and the rope. Strolling up to her he offered an outstretched hand and from his lips one simple command "Up". She took his hand and pulled herself up to stand in front of him. His hand slid down her body lightly as he bent down and picked up one of the ropes. With practiced hands he slowly uncoiled the length of rope and ran it through his hands enjoying its texture in his palms. Moving behind her, his hand slid around her body leaving a trail of rope across her skin. Instinctively, she raised her arms so not to hinder his caressing movements, or the ever-growing cocoon of rope that encased her body...

The Taking (resistance)

With a purposeful stride he entered the room, a coil of rope dangled from one of his strong hands. She waited for him at the other end of the room. As he stepped towards her, she instinctively took a step back. Realizing what she was doing, she stopped and took a step forward her face set defiantly. He unraveled the rope as he continued towards her leaving a trail snaking behind him. She strode towards him and they met in the middle of the room. As they stared into each other's eyes his hands moved to encircle her with the rope only to have the rope stop short. His eyes traveled down the rope to find her foot firmly planted on it. He turned his eyes back to her face questioningly. She smiled and shrugged in answer, but didn't move her foot. As he reached out to pull her off balance she darted back a few steps out of his reach and slide into a fighter's crouch.

So the challenge had been offered and the game had changed. He lunged forward and snatched at her arm, but she quickly twisted her arm free as she scurried out of reach. They smiled at each other wickedly and then he started moving towards her, slowly this time, carefully trying to herd her into a corner of the room. With a burst of speed she made a bolt for the closing gap between him and the wall. His hand shot out, his grip locked tight around her wrist and moments later their bodies collided in a frenzy of movement before crashing to the floor. Suddenly she felt her arm forced into an unnatural position. A wave of pain rose through her body encouraging her to be still as any movement only seemed to increase the intensity of the pain. As the rope wrapped around her wrist it bit into her skin. She struggled to break free as she felt the rope wrap around her again and again, biting deep into her flesh slowly forcing her into helplessness...

These two styles are not independent of each other, but more like two ends of a sliding scale where they blend with each other in varying degrees. Both of these styles are parts of how I interact with others when it comes to rope bondage, and my hope is that you see a mirror in them to your own journey as well. Let's have a closer look at each of these styles and the reasons why I do them. You may have your own reasons as well that I have not thought of.

I'll start off with The Giving style because it is the most common rope bondage scene that I see explored.

The Giving (non resistance)

- TRUST — This deeply important part of rope bondage is key to this type of interaction. To give over to the experience and trust in the Top requires trusting the Top. There are of course various levels of trust, from "I trust you to put a piece around me" to "I trust you to swing a chainsaw around me while I'm completely bound." The chainsaw level of trust is not needed for exploring The Giving.

- CONTROL — Control is another core aspect. Whether I'm tying someone to the bed, spread wide or a simple chest harness, there is always a level of control that I have been granted or acquired over time from my bottom. Rope is a reminder of the control that has been surrendered to me.

- CONTACT — Bodies need to be close to one another for bondage to take place, and through this closeness breath can be felt and touch lingers. Bondage can break through the personal space barriers in our culture, and in a way it gives you an excuse to touch each other that might not have had permission before.

- PASSION/INTIMACY — Rope can become an extension of a touch or caress that stays for a length of time on the bottom's body, the vibration of rope transmitting from one person how they feel about the other. It can assist in the connection between people both as the rope becomes a link between them, and through the contact of bodies that rope bondage causes.

- MEDITATION — For the Top meditation can be through focusing on the details of a tie or by not focusing and just doing. It is similar for the bottom where they can focus on each individual aspect of what is happening or just let all the sensations flow over them.

- HEALING — I find that emotional healing is something that can happen with The Giving form of rope bondage on various levels, from a healing of both people involved to that of just one individual. The most common form I've seen is the healing of the bottom who uses the bondage to drop their emotional guards and allow themselves to experience and express the emotions hidden deep inside them, especially things like grief.

- CREATIVITY — Though I can be creative in The Taking, practice has shown me that non-resistance bondage due to the relaxed atmosphere that naturally occurs. It allows your focus to work the ideas with limited distraction. It can also allow for the bottom to give feedback in ways that can lead to the bondage becoming an artistic collaboration between partners.

- FUN — This is one of the most important aspects non-resistance bondage to me. I believe that all scenes, no matter how formal, serious, demanding, painful or testing should be fun in the end. Sure it might not be a barrel of laughs at the time but when you think back, see your rope marks or feel your sore muscles, I'd be surprised if a smile didn't cross your lips. I would question any sort of play that in the end doesn't create some form of fun, happiness, or bliss.

The Taking (resistance)

- TRUST — Trust is also a core aspect when it comes to resistance bondage. The level of trust needed tends to be more than for non-resistance due to the fact that it is easier for things to escalate to dangerous levels when struggling and fighting happens. However, it is often through the work in The Giving that this trust can be built. It is not an instant thing.

- CONTROL — If you are the Top, there is the control of the bottom, which is usually fought to gain in resistance bondage, and you must also work to control the scene or situation. For both the Top and the bottom there is also the deeply important element of self-control. The level of control needed depends on the level of resistance in the play, as well as the level of focus that can be dedicated by the partner who is retaining control in the scene. If a bottom has lost self-control, the Top needs to maintain focus even more.

- PASSION — While the passion in non-resistance leans towards being a thing of intimacy, in resistance bondage it leans towards being a thing of primal emotions. These primal passions and emotions don't blend together but rather clash with each other in a struggle for dominance. They build up off each other, until one final breaks, and the two roles, victor and victim, are set for that moment. At this point these primal passions will run the strongest and deepest.

- BODY KNOWLEDGE — Both the Top and the bottom learn a lot about their own body, and the other person they are, in The Taking. Body control then grows from body knowledge, because only by being able to understand what is happening, and the limits of each body, can a person then control either their own or another's without causing damage. From my own experiences, I have learned how to better interpret the way a body feels in my hands. Also I have become more aware of my body and how to move it.

- EXERCISE — Personal experience has taught me that resistance bondage can be a great workout. I'm sure this might not be an aspect that many care much about, but if you're after some exercise, rolling around with someone and getting hot and sweaty sure can be a fun way to do it!

- SKILL GROWTH — Resistance bondage has a little twist to classic skill building, because as a Top, the more times you play with a bottom, the more the bottom will learn your skills and how to counter them. So the result is that the bottom will become more and more challenging and so you are challenged to constantly improve yourself.

- FUN — Just as with non-resistance bondage, I feel that fun is a core aspect of resistance bondage. Sure things can get intense, bodies and even minds can be pushed to their limits, but in the end you should have enjoyed yourself on some level. To me play is about mutual gain and pleasure.

I hope by examining both The Giving and The Taking you have opened your eyes to other aspects of the wonderful world of rope bondage, or maybe just confirmed some of your own thoughts. The break-down of power can also go back and forth between these two styles as the paths to our final destinations wind in different ways. Remember that while resistance bondage can be quite demanding, it does not mean that non-resistance in turn is not just because I examined it as The Giving. There are many sides of non-resistance bondage that can be both physically and/or mentally demanding, like predicament bondage, semi and full suspension, and even some of the positions or lengths of time the body is rope bondage.

I wish you all an amazing rope journey through life.

THOUGHTS ON ROPE, SUBMISSION AND FEMINISM

by Madison Young

(1)

Queer. Feminist. Submissive. Rope Slut. These are a few of the words that I embrace as part of my identity. As a queer identified person I've always been more aggressive around my sexuality.

If you are queer, you are queer no matter who you are having sex with and you are engaging in queer sex because it is part of your identity. If you are a kinky rope slut, that is still an element of your identity even when engaging in vanilla sex. If you are a feminist, you are engaging in sex positive feminist bondage because this is a part of your identity. You are aware of it, embrace it, and are ultimately in control of the sex and bdsm you are engaging in. You play with power structures because of your strong sense of self.

I knew that I didn't want what other girls wanted. Instead I wanted other girls. This was the catalyst for me to be active in my sexuality and my identity rather than being passive and following the ebb and flow of the world around me in small town Ohio. My sexuality and identity were always something that I had to fight for and to educate others about. It was part of my politics. My aggressiveness in my queer identity translated to aggressiveness in my claiming of my submission and, at the same time, a profound freedom in rope bondage. I have a deep desire for intense sensation. Just as some desire the light touch of a hand grazing across their body, I desire the deep thud of a 2x4 and rope hugging tight across my breasts restricting my breath and bringing me closer to orgasm.

The rope wrapped tightly around my body. So very tight. I could feel in that rope every bear hug that I ever gave my cousins and kids on the school yard. Bear hugs that were so tight it could send them running. Send them into a fit of tears. So tight like I would grab on to my teachers leg in 1st and 2nd grade not wanting them to leave for the summer. So tight when I was a 6 year old girl, I would grab onto my father and sob for him not to leave. Hold on tight. I could smell the scent of my father's sweatshirt after work that would linger with rope fibers and leaf bits, the touch of his callused hands and the bristle from his bearded cheeks. I felt those memories those scents, wrapped tightly around me. Biting into me. It felt safe like home. I would never let go and neither would they. I felt secure in their presence, in the rope.

It was like falling in love fast and hard. There was some pain involved as your body manipulated itself in this hold to adjust for another being. But the entire time you know that it will hurt much more to part with your lover,the rope. That it will break your heart to exist without its presence. It was comforting. A place of warmth and security. A place that I believed in, that I belonged to. And I never really wanted to leave.

Why do we engage in rope bondage as a tool with in Ds? Why is it fascinating and erotically stimulating to engage in power exchange and to disassemble power structures that have been put in place by a social normative? We are breaking the rules. As queers, as feminists, as kinky persons, and sexual outlaws we have always been breaking the rules. We go outside of the designated sexual norms as we search for connection, community, and fulfillment in our sexual lives and identities. Our sexual selves were not handed to us, so we have eroticized the disassembling of traditional power structures and protocols and have built our own to use as our sex toys.

In the relationship in which I serve, rope is used as a treat or a reward for good behavior. In this way rope is largely used to gain power over me as a submissive and to motivate my behavior. I know that if I do as I'm told I will be rewarded with rope.

I'm a rope fetishist and get off on the scent, the touch, the taste, the bite of rope. I often think of rope as a fine wine and a personal fantasy of mine is to attend an event structured as a "rope tasting," similar to a wine tasting. I'm still waiting for this to happen, so if one is assembled please do send me an invite.

Rope can also be used in order to engage in sadistic and masochistic pleasures by inflicting "pain" on the submissive. Examples include quick and painful suspensions that are not meant for sustainability, tight nipple bondage, and predicament bondage situations. Take-downs and strict bondage that pushes the body to extreme situations (such as extreme back arching) can be quite painful, challenging and absolutely delicious options for using rope within power play.

Rope is a language used by sadists and masochists while fulfilling one another's desires and creating connection amongst our community and a conduit for socialization within our alternative views of sexuality. Rope acts as a tool for us to physically dialogue with our partner; a language for those of us that have no need for words, only action. It is an intimate dance, exploring one another's bodies, our forms, the space around us, and even our physical limitations. Rope is a connection within the indifference of life, through and with our differences.

I knew from the time that I started socializing with other children that I was different. Education and the arts would be my ticket to a larger community of people where I might find connection. By high school I had convinced my parents to release me into a performing arts school in downtown Cincinnati to study theater. I was determined to find connection and community and a sense of self amongst the chaos of art. Although there was some struggle along the way, I did find what I was looking for.

I found it on a stage cracked open in front of hundreds of audience members. Stripped away of all ego and left open and vulnerable we learned how to allow for connection with other performers in front of an audience. We learned how to share energy with one another. We learned what it meant to be centered, grounded, to be in our bodies and out of our heads. We learned how to be a conduit for art and energy and how to allow these things to run into and out of our bodies, our mouths, our fingertips. We learned how to create art with a purpose, and how our actions are loaded with intention and purpose.

I take these simple lessons with me through life in everything that I do; yoga, tantra, service, submission, sex, masochism, rope play, writing, teaching, and performance.

I've taken it upon myself as a mission to embrace my queer feminist self and my submissive rope slut self and to share that with the world and the way that these two worlds coincide.

(2)

Submission; yielding to someone; obedience; compliance

Sex positive feminism embraces the entire range of human sexuality and bases itself on the idea that sexual freedom is an essential component of women's freedom. BDSM is based around power and sensation play with a strong emphasis on communication and consent. Submissives engaging in this kind of consensual sexual activity are validating their sexuality through the act of their submission and, at the same time, taking control and embracing their sexuality.

I made my way to the locker room, clothing soaked and sticking to my flesh. I peeled off my layers, my onion bits. Layers of determination, a hard outer shell of armor protecting a soft bodied vulnerable creature. Purple splotches, green & yellowing thumbprints & finger marks raised & red tiger stripes across my chest up & down my thighs worn proudly like a badge of courage, like a flag, while the other women in the locker room stare and whisper to their friends.

I concern my doctor. She worries about the bruises. She worries that maybe this is not consensual. This is most definitely consensual.

Leaning against a bedpost ass jutted out and begging for a thick wooden 2x4 piece of lumber to come crashing down on my eager porcelain flesh. My hands are generously tied with fragrant jute rope in front of me so that I might hold the vibrating Hitachi against my sopping-wet cunt. The 2x4 comes down in a thunderous smack against my ass, a deep hard thud. So deep and so hard that I feel like the flesh of my ass might swallow the long wooden implement and be absorbed into my bloodstream.

"Thank you Sir" I scream out in ecstasy. Vibrator pressed tight against my cunt, heart racing waves of orgasmic warmth rush through my body sent from Josh's wooden stick that is hitting one solid home run after another.

My body boils with pleasure, is overcome with pleasure. Greedy & needy for even more. Driven to insanity. I am a madwoman crazy and wanting for just one more hard strike of the 2x4, hard & firm & reliable; a stable dependable thud that has my pussy dripping desire down my spread thighs. Just one more rush from the lumberyard. One more crashing down. Please I will do anything for just one more for my insatiable cunt that will always be screaming for just one more. Yes. Yes this is consensual.

There is perception that submissives are weak, that they feel like they have done something to be punished. This is a misconception. Submissives are often strong and powerful wo/men who wish to set aside or to give their "power" to another person. Submissives are willing to make themselves vulnerable, open to experiences. They serve and give something back to both their community and to the one(s) they serve. Their service and education can result in both personal growth and community development. Submissives are there to better the lives of others and in doing so it enriches their own lives. Submissives are there to express gratitude, to make the one(s) in which s(he) serves look good, and to be a role model with in his/her community.

In serving a dominant the submissive is not only serving the individual but is also given an opportunity to pay respect to a leather history that has existed for decades. The greater the understanding a submissive has of this history the more layers and depth that are attached to any single act of submission whether it be a caning, service, following protocol, or experiencing the wrath of a punishment. This punishment is an indicator of not only disrespect or willful disobedience to an individual, but to a community, to a history, and to something that is much larger than us.

I wished I could disappear & was thankful for the inviting darkness that the blindfold brought. I was led downstairs to the dungeon, and placed on a suspended table which was disorienting and difficult to balance on without sight. I awaited my first punishment on all fours. Presenting my ass. Rope biting around my chest, under my arms, pressed up against my rib cage, attempting to take over my breath and lead me into submission.

I would hear at later events that there was quite the line that had formed. Everyone wanted their turn. Flogs, paddles, hands, straps, belts, clamps, clothespins, men's & women's mouths and implements. I gently cooed and with a "thank you Sir," "thank you Ma'am." I changed positions presenting my chest, my pussy, rotating to give onlookers a better view. I stood in difficult stress positions squatting balancing, blindfolded. Head spinning, chasing after the texture of voices in the room. Negotiations with Josh as he would hand me over to the next participant, each politely asking "if this is too hard, could I go harder?" "If it pleases you Sir." "You seem like such a good girl," they would say. "What could you have possibly done to deserve this punishment?" "I'm not at liberty to say, Sir. I'm sorry Sir."

Over the knee and ass out, pussy out, head high. I followed the words like light, like butterflies. I let the sensation wipe through me, the sensations of seasoned leather men and dominants and newbies who were shy and nervous. You would have thought they were the ones under the whip.

I could feel a community around me young and old, SMers, experimenters and swingers. Each with a different stroke, a different touch. Polite and grateful for taking part in my punishment and I imparted my gratitude to them.

Mr. Royal approached whispering in my ear. "Just one more and I'll take you home."

"Thank you Sir."

This swing was familiar. The cane struck my ass, that had already started to bruise with hours of punishment. But I welcomed this touch. His touch.

Count and show me you're sorry.

One. I'm sorry Sir. Please Sir forgive me.

Two. Sir, I'm so very sorry Sir, I will be more mindful of my behavior Sir.

Three. Sir, I'm sorry Sir. I will only show the greatest of respect to us and our protocol Sir.

I felt tired and broken. Worn down but at the same time fulfilled. I felt an unselfish pleasure from a job well done.

"You did good tonight Maddie. I'm very proud of you. You made a lot of people very happy.

"Thank you Sir."

(3)

In one's journey of submission one acquires certain skill sets that are valuable in their daily experiences with both bdsm and service. Some concepts and skill sets that are useful include being familiar with visualization, the use of breath, the concept of energy and charkas, what it means to be present and in ones body and the ability to release. These are all concepts that I came to know before having much experience in bdsm. My interest in tantra, yoga and the arts all heavily influenced the way that I approached bdsm and submission. This influence can be seen when the one I serve is gifting me with energy as s(he) is caning my feet. I feel my feet heat up with energy. I can feel the energy as the color red, then purple, and finally blue. I allow the energy to melt up my calves, my thighs and drip into the well of my cunt, where it churns and then is released in breath or in orgasm . . . if I am allowed. This is how submissives can do things such as cum from a caning or a whipping or the intense sensation of rope during a suspension. It is simply a redirection of energy that is entering the body.

D/s; playing with power and trust in an erotic way

To completely give oneself over to another, to serve another, to embrace obedience like a lover, puts a submissive into a vulnerable and humbled state of being. It feels safe, warm, and comforting; a womb-like environment. To be keenly aware of your sexual desires, those of others, and to act in an unselfish manner will result in more than your own orgasm. You will be able to feel fully connected to another person and be fully dedicated to their pleasure. An excitement washes over me when I am following rules, partaking in protocol. I can feel the desires and rules that have been set for me rubbing up against my body like fragrant rope. This internal bondage sets me free, allowing me movement to test and taste the sweetness and meaning behind each rule and ritual.

His ropes will bite in to me causing me pleasure & pain. He will find my buttons to push and it won't take him very long because he knows me. He knows how I work and he has read my manual & I am simple toy to play with. And soon I will learn that our bdsm play isn't entirely for me or my pleasure. I will learn about compromise and service. But not yet not like this.

Rope

I often personify rope. It is my lover, my special treat. I try not to become too greedy for its fragrance, its bite, its taste which lingers in my mouth. Within rope I find home. The tighter its embrace the more I coo as I float off into cotton candy sweetness. I am freed from my body as I embrace the space around me. I usually regard by body as a clunky piece of equipment that I'm forced to drag around on a daily basis. Rope allows all of who I am not, all physical and mental restriction, to slip away and leaves only the core of my being. I am shown to be my most vulnerable and truest self, cracked wide open for a genuine and profound exchange with the one that I serve.

My experiences with in bdsm and submission have enriched my life and given room for me to feel on a deeper level. I embrace my submission and feel empowered and humbled at the same time by these experiences. I feel that any woman who is embracing her sexuality and actively pursuing genuine pleasure for both herself and her partners is participating in a form of feminism.

What do you love more than anything, slut?

Rope sir.

Rope will only be given to you here as a reward. You will have to earn it. Do you think you can do that slut?

Yes sir. I will do my best sir.

That's a good slut.

Italicized text drawn from Madison Young's "Tail of a Bondage Model"

BONDAGE FOR PEOPLE, NOT PARCELS

by Esinem / Bruce Argue

In all of my years exploring rope, the most important thing that I have discovered about bondage is that it should not be like wrapping a parcel. It is not simply a matter of being able to tie a particular knot, or replicate a specific tie exactly. It should be done with feeling and create an energy flow with your partner. Too often I find that people become distracted by learning elaborate knots, discussing rope and other technicalities at the expense of this. Bondage is more about the way that you do it, rather than what you do or what materials are used. However, this does not mean that safety, good technique and appropriate equipment are not vital.

I would compare a bondage scene to a passionate dance like the tango — you're in very close contact with your partner, one of you leads and the other follows, and together you produce something magical. If one were to merely follow the steps laid out in a dance instruction manual, the dance could be millimeter perfect but, without passion, it would be nothing more than a mechanical exercise and emotionally dead. Bondage is no different. Sadly, many people miss the point. They fail to make the emotional connection and end up becoming detached, merely "wrapping parcels". Binding your lover should not be a destination to be reached, but a journey to be enjoyed and savored.

I have found a wide variety of ways to avoid "wrapping parcels" over the years. If I am tying somebody for the first time, I try to get an idea of what will push their buttons and discover from which perspective they approach bondage. Are they drawn to rope for SM, D/s, M/s, or as a sensual experience? As with any form of BDSM or sexual activity, I have found that if I go down the wrong avenue, I will have a loser from the start. The situation will usually determine how I come to my conclusions.

If I already know the person to some extent, I might have some insights into their tastes from conversations, a web profile or watching them play with others. However, sometimes I am asked to tie somebody in a club who I have not met before that moment. In these instances, I might whisper in their ear where between "soft and sensual" to "hard and nasty" their preferences lie. Other times, I rely on non-verbal cues, such as demeanor and reactions.

For example, when I encounter bratty subs who want to fight back a little or try to escape, they tend to respond to a more forceful approach before finally submitting. Usually, with this type of interaction, my bondage will become opportunistic and struggling limbs will be pinned and roped in whatever position they present themselves. I enjoy the challenge of this sort of encounter and the opportunities for mischief it presents; even though it is invariably not a question of who will win but when they will lose. It always has that exhilaration that comes with any sort of play fighting. On the other hand, the ones that drop their eyes, offer their wrists to be tied and act submissively are more likely to be compliant, allowing me to decide on positions for tying.

The way they react to touch is also a good clue. My most simple Litmus test is to grab a good handful of hair and draw the head back. Their reaction to this simple move speaks volumes. I am not the only one who has used a test like this. Almost 30 years ago in the Japanese magazine "Venus" Akechi Denki (one of the greatest of modern shibari masters, teachers and performers who passed away in 2005) was quoted as saying "I can usually find whether a girl has an M [submissive] side or not. When meeting, one of the ways of finding out is by grabbing her hair and pulling her down slowly to the ground."

Just like in good sex, one pays attention to feedback and builds on that feedback. When that feedback is positive, keep following the trail of clues where they lead, and when the feedback is negative, pull back and reexamine what messages might have been misinterpreted. Some sessions will be tender, sensual and loving bringing out the deepest connections. Others will be like doing battle. Others still will be frivolous affairs, with a certain amount of teasing, laughter, frustration, play fighting and ultimately satisfaction at having rendered them helpless. I recall the reaction of a Japanese bondage artist to watching me engaged in a scene that involved the latter. She was somewhat bemused as bondage in Japan always seems quite a serious affair. Her comment was: "You two were really having fun, weren't you?" to which, I replied, "If we're not having fun, what's the point?"

During any scene, I always try to be aware of the body language, breathing and the look in their eyes, even if I have played with them before. Whilst learning and observation can improve matters, some of it will still come down to intuition and luck. Passionate bondage is not an exact science. It cannot be achieved only by book or formal learning. Communication is another key, whether verbal or non-verbal. Both sides spell out what is working and what is not in a positive and constructive way can also be helpful to this end, allowing each scene the opportunity to be improved.

Sometimes everything will click intuitively, other times it will not, regardless of the skill of the rigger. There is no magic formula that works every time. It is simply a question of improving the odds and, ultimately, it will rest on the chemistry between the two of you. It certainly helps to be tying a true rope-slut, who goes into ecstasy as the mere thought of being tied, and I find this almost invariably makes for a more rewarding session. After all, lack of enthusiasm is the only thing more infectious than enthusiasm.

Another tool to consider is positions. The pose I tie someone in can have dramatic effects on the bottom psychologically. For example, ties where the genitals are exposed, and the bottom is unable to hide or protect them, can create shame, embarrassment, vulnerability (especially in the case of men unable to guard the testicles) or uneasiness. Playing on the sense of embarrassment seems to be a key element in the Japanese approach, where the concept of shame is particularly intense culturally. This style, which can be seen in much of Yukimura Haruki's, is called "shuuchi-nawa", shuuchi = shyness, bashfulness and nawa = rope. In my experience, some Japanese girls exhibit an unique demeanor which delightfully combines this demureness with intensive submissiveness. However, this is not the easy stereotype it might seem. My understanding is that in Japan, the game is played a little differently with safe-words being uncommon, the sub giving up all control to the rope top and it being a matter of honor not to back down during a scene.

Other positions can be largely practical. I might want to secure somebody to a piece of dungeon furniture, a bed or in a suitable pose for a particular activity, be it sex or play. Perhaps I would like to enforce a concept of servility — in which case, I can put my partner in a bowed or kneeling pose. If I want to push them into a sense of imbalance or fear, I can destabilize them by lifting one leg off the ground, which can create a constant battle within themselves that some bottoms find quite disturbing. Obviously, you need to make sure that they cannot actually fall by securing the bondage to a suspension point, or by some other method. Adding a blindfold to the equation can also be an extremely potent tool for enforcing an emotion through the way they are tied.

Predicament ties, such as putting a leg into a stressful position then connecting that line to a nipple clamp or hair bondage, can a deliciously sadistic element. However, one should never underestimate the effect of time, which can lead to moments of extreme submission for even the most hardy and recalcitrant. This fact was known to the originators of Japanese bondage who used stress positions in torture, punishment and interrogation long before they became a tool for eroticism.

The order of restraint is also significant for me. In order to assert dominance, I believe that one should take control immediately and assertively when tying. Even for the most sensuous scene, I like to begin by grasping the wrists to move them into position and maintaining a grip until the first wrap secures them. This gives the message straight away that I am in control and clearly indicates that the session has begun. It is an important psychological moment and one that has more significance than meekly offered wrists or patiently waiting for them to be tied while other bondage is completed. It is well worth mastering the technique of achieving this step slickly and quickly.

Most impressions are made in the first 30 seconds, and I believe this applies to bondage as well. It is the equivalent to a firm handshake, compared to the limp, "wet-fish" variety or a strong opening in dance. Start by creating a positive reaction, not a negative, or even neutral, one. Simple details such as being able to smoothly flick out a coil of rope without tangles can make a huge difference. If you are fumbling this initial tie or spending ages trying to untangle a rat's nest of rope, you can easily lose the moment and are unlikely to give the impression of a competent rope top. An opening move I love is when I have a hank of rope stored in a half-bow and, taking an end in either hand, I can look into my sub's eyes and snap the hank undone. It unequivocally says "I mean business", makes a powerful statement and creates a clear beginning.

I like to think of the rope as an extension of my hands. This mindset is probably the most important in avoiding "wrapping parcels". I like to be purposeful in my handling and mindful of the routing of the rope in order to maximize the erotic potential, both in terms of providing sensuality and avoiding unintentional discomfort, just as I do with my hands. By being in control of the rope, I am constantly aware of what the whole rope is doing, especially those flailing loose ends. If one is not on top of this, it is easy to lose the mood by causing rope burn by pulling badly routed rope too fast, pinching the skin or allowing the end to whip up into the face. A little attention, a guarding hand and lifting bindings to create room to pull through can avoid this.

In terms of application, I have discovered many nuances. The first is the degree of firmness used to apply the rope. I usually keep some tension on the rope at all times. Not only does this prevent the wraps slipping, but more importantly, it focuses the sub's attention on the deliberateness of the binding and how liberty is slowly being removed. Depending on the sensation I wish to create, this might be a gentle or strong tension. Unlike parcels, people are aware of these feelings. To me, maintaining this is vital and I feel that I am relinquishing control and losing connection if I relax this tension.

A further factor is the degree of decisiveness. My movements can be almost dream-like in a soft and sensual scene, yet they might be more abrupt and forceful if dominance and control is the objective. In both instances, tempo is also important. The former example would usually be slow paced, whereas the latter might be faster. Subconsciously I will often fall into step with whatever music is playing, but the mood of the scene will also be a big influence — which is the more significant tends to depend upon whether it is a performance or private play. As with any erotic process I engage in, I attempt to build incrementally to a crescendo. This might be by upping the tempo and/or gradually increasing the tension of the bindings or degree of restriction. I might employ varying tempos during the process; for example, wrapping slowly, yet completing tie-offs rapidly. This places more emphasis on the wrapping, which is the more tactile element, and reduces the time spent on the less tactile tie-offs, whilst providing a contrast between the feel of the two actions.

Osada Steve, one of the world's top kinbakushi, uses an interesting combination of techniques. He will move quickly and decisively to apply a body wrap, yet he will "pull the punch" by deliberately relaxing to complete the move. It looks savage, but is deceptively soft, whilst nicely accentuating the action. Another technique he taught me was to tug knots and turns, again adding punctuation to one's actions. I use both of these tricks frequently now as I feel they emphasize the act of tying and process of restriction.

A complimentary component is the degree of smoothness. I usually try to create an uninterrupted flow. Smoothness is far easier to achieve with the right length of rope. The magic length is equivalent to four times the span of one's outstretched arms. This allows the rope to be pulled through in a single movement, assuming it is used doubled in kinbaku style, rather than a clumsy hand over hand like a sailor hauling up an anchor. However, the real secret is practicing until your brain is hardly aware of what you are doing and your muscles have learned the process of tying. A perfect example of this muscle memory is the way if you ask the driver of a stick shift where reverse is, he will probably mimic the motion with the gear shift hand before answering. His hand remembers what his mind no longer needs to be conscious of.

Once my mind became free of having to think about what I was doing, I began to tie intuitively, carried along on the flow of the scene and not being distracted by the practical aspects. With practice, it can become an uninterrupted process without indecisive moments to break the hypnotic effect.

It is when my mind is freed in this way that the activity becomes almost meditative and the sense of "oneness" is most apparent. Nothing else exists beyond the here and now. Even in a busy and noisy club, all distraction drops away and I have frequently been unable to even say what music was playing, let alone answer somebody's question about what I thought of the DJ.

Consider also that you cannot successfully tango at arms length. Bondage can thus be one of the more physically contact intensive areas of SM. You are not distanced in the same way that you might be by a whip or flogger. Body contact makes the whole experience intimate. There is a massive difference between standing two feet away to tie and sitting with your partner between your thighs and reaching around, holding them close, whilst you slowly wind rope around their body. Parcels don't care, but for many people, the turn on is the embrace of the rope. How much more powerful is this when combined with a physical embrace?

Again, as in dance, how you choose to use physical contact will influence the mood. It can be soft or aggressive, seductive or dominant, it can even be teasingly withdrawn. As an integral part of this, one's whole demeanour should be appropriate. I am not of the school of poker-faced Japanese rope-masters with their ubiquitous dark glasses, which appear to hide the last vestiges of emotion. From my perspective, it appears rope is usually a serious business for them. I suspect the image of the inscrutable, apparently emotionless dominant is a favorite role. However, I prefer to draw on a wider range of emotions and share those with my partner. Choosing the demeanor that matches your intention is of great importance.

Good bondage is not just about creating a work of art and then sitting back to admire your handiwork. Admittedly, simply "gift wrapping" might be the name of the game for a photo shoot but I am discussing real bondage scenes. This is not to say that I don't enjoy the aesthetics, part of the joy of good rope work is the way it can enhance the beauty of the person I am tying. I find a more dynamic and interactive scene, where there is some tying and re-tying, more fulfilling. A common mistake is to think a scene is over once a particular tie has been created and to forget that untying can be just as erotic as tying. It should be a conscious process receiving the same degree of attention as the tying. Unless there is a good reason, such as it being appropriate to a role play, removing rope should be a leisurely business to ensure a smooth landing from sub-space. If the untying is rushed, it can be as unerotic as having bedding suddenly ripped away on a cold morning.

My interpretation of bondage is not simply "a means of restraint". It should become a medium of exchange and communication. The key to this is to understand your partner's needs and meet them through a combination of physical contact, mindful rope handling and, above all, passion. If you cannot transport your partner to Cloud-9 with a little rope, some simple ties and a lot of feeling, adding more rope, learning exotic technical skills or suspension will never make them fly. Learning to create that magical connection is the most important skill and the one which will make your rope scenes special. I have found that when thinking of binding people not parcels, Japanese photographer and kinbakushi Araki sums it all up perfectly when he tells his models "I'm binding your heart, not your body".

THE WAY OF A ZEN ROPE MASTER

by JD of Two Knotty Boys

Two monks arrived at a torrential river. At the river's edge stood a woman anxiously watching the water pass before her.

"I didn't think the river would rise so fast," the woman commented to the monks. "Now I have no way of getting across."

Without hesitation one of the monks picked up the woman, slung her over a shoulder and walked her across the river, setting her down on the other side.

A look of shock flashed across the face of the other monk as he watched on from a distance. The helpful monk waved goodbye to the woman, crossed the river once again and returned to the other monk's side. From there the two monks walked off together.

As the monks walked side-by-side the helpful monk whistled, while the others monk's face grew red with increasing anger until he suddenly exclaimed, "You do realize by touching that woman you broke our monastic rules?"

"I do," the helpful monk calmly replied. "But I set her down on the other side of the river and you're still holding on to her."

———

The parable of the two monks illustrates the fundamental difference between those who seek insight and mastery though rational creeds or revealed scriptures, and those who seek insight through direct experience and compassionate response. That is, there are those who hold tight to ritual and protocol and feel a sense of wrongness the more they or another diverge from a pre-described way; and there are those whose ways are more flexible, more attuned to the moment and the needs of the now. These latter people might be said to be more Zen. And, when these same people express their nature in the context of a sensual rope bondage exchange, it could further be said they exhibit the way of a Zen rope master.

If I were to present a suitable and accurate explanation of Zen. I would gather all those who were interested into a classroom, stand quietly behind a podium for five minutes and then leave. Doing so would not, as it might first appear, be an effort to conceal or confuse the meaning of Zen. It would merely constitute a more direct exposition of what is meant by Zen, an example that would surpass a verbal treatise on the subject. Nevertheless, I'm unable to do such a thing and if I was, most would feel cheated by such an experience, so I present the following brief explanation of Zen as a means of achieving sensual dominance, mastery of rope and connection with others.

The word Zen is the Japanese way of pronouncing the Chinese word Chán, which in turn is the Chinese way of pronouncing the Sanskrit word dhyāna; and dhyāna, regretfully, is a very difficult word to translate into English. Despite this fact, scholars have attempted to understand dhyāna by referring to it as "mediation". But in truth it is not simply mediation. Others have called it "contemplation", a more accurate description than meditation; still contemplation does not fully encapsulate dhyāna's meaning either. So it is that we do not have a clear English definition of dhyāna, Chán or Zen. Nevertheless, experience provides understanding of what these terms mean, or, more specifically, what Zen is.

For example, most of us have ridden a bicycle. We did so as children and many of us still do so as adults. When riding a bicycle you are doing something, actively engaging the pedals and the handlebars, steering and looking around. You don't think about it once you know how to ride; you simply do it without thought or regard. You loose yourself in the riding, your hands, feet, legs and arms working in concert to achieve a course or a destination, while your mind drifts off in thought. Essentially you become one with the bicycle. As the bicycle moves, you move. Is the cyclist riding the bicycle or is the bicycle riding the cyclist? This is Zen. The same thing can be said when you have an excellent dance partner. Who leads? Who follows? When seen from a distance, two people dancing can appear to move as one, elegantly gliding and spinning across the floor. This too is Zen.

The question then becomes, how do I achieve oneness, or "Zen", with my partner in the context of a sensual rope bondage exchange? Or, put another way, how do I achieve a dominant presence that supersedes active contemplation of my actions, so that I might tie while remaining open and present to the person I am with?

The first step toward answering these questions is to realize that your experience of the world and your relationship with others (sensual or otherwise) directly correlates to your state of mind. Your mind and the sensual receptivity of your partner are interdependent. If you possess a negative mind, a mind that sees the world as a myriad of disappointments and letdowns, you will experience negative partners who disappoint and let you down. If you consider your rope skills lacking or feel practice is futile on account you're "just not good at tying rope," your rope skill will be lacking and practice will be futile. This will be so because your mind is so powerful, it makes it so.

On the other hand, if you live your life with a positive attitude, and you recognize that your skills are a process and not a static quality, if you embrace your mind's power to manifest all that you experience, then you will see positive results to your efforts and your sensual world will transform. So it is, as difficult as it may be to accept, there are no answers "out there". There are no gurus who can give you what you need. All your answers, all the wisdom necessary to achieve a conscious, directed and skilled dominant disposition is within you. Once you know this—not "believe" this—but know this to the core of your bones, you will possess awareness unlike any other you have known before. This awareness will end your estrangement from the world and help your relationship with your partner blossom. Together you and your partner will be able to play like the skillfully dancing couple—the movements of two seen as one. Knowing your mind is interdependent with the sensual receptivity of your partner is only the first step toward achieving the way. There are other steps that need to be taken as well.

Letting go of your attachment to perfection is the second step, and if taken, it is this step that will mark the most notable shift in your disposition. Imagine a rigger who arrives at a play party with his partner in hand. He is anxious to tie and show all that he has been practicing, and his partner is excited to be tied and to experience his skill.

The rigger finds a station at which he can tie, a St. Andrew's cross, and begins to work. Before long his partner is bound to the cross, but the Karada he recently learned and tied across his partner's torso isn't looking like the one he'd studied. It looks crooked to him and so he unties it and has a second go at it. His second attempt turns into a third and he starts to become noticeably agitated. "Why can't I get my Karada to look like the instructor's looked?" he grumbles under his breath as he undoes his tie and has a fourth go at it. Meanwhile his partner is growing bored and feeling ignored, and so speaks out, "It doesn't matter. Look at me, let's just play." But the rigger keeps tying, unable to stop his struggle for perfection, unable to redefine his efforts as practice and, in turn, unable to connect with his partner. He is fixated on perfection and for his fixation he is distant and his partner is growing increasingly more distant from him.

The story of the obsessed rigger illustrates how perfection can become a source of suffering. To desire the achievement of an idealized tie is not to recognize the fact that so long as there is not a safety issue associated with it, all ties are ideal—even the messy ones. Letting go of a tie looking or feeling a certain way allows a rigger to experience more of their partner, more of the person they came to connect with, and potentially love. The abandonment of perfection might at first glance seem like a recipe for poor skills, for a person who will never learn or never reach an admired level of skill. The opposite is true, but such knowledge can only be realized if you take the second step...and let go of perfection.

The third step toward achieving the way is recognizing and refraining from habitual behaviors that sabotage your efforts or contradict your better judgment. It offers a counterpoint to letting go of your attachment to perfection. Many of us are very good at sabotaging and contradicting ourselves because we have had years of practice at it. We have become very skilled at projecting negativity, frustration, loss of patience or anger. Because of how much you've practiced behaviors such as these, it takes a long time to subdue their influence on your life. Still, by remaining conscious to the triggers and the moments when you start to feel these habitual behaviors rise in your mind, you can breathe through their pull. This pull, more often that not, leads to making matters worse, rather than better.

The fourth and final step in the process to achieving the way is compassion. Compassion, I know, may seem antithetical to a dominant disposition. Still it is compassion, above and beyond all other qualities, that will solidify your link with your partner. Through compassion you will become a safe container for your partner to open up within. A place where your partner is comfortable under what, for most, might be disagreeable circumstances. Bound and immobilized, your partner must know he or she is with someone who can be trusted, someone who will stop play or untie a piece at the first sign of *bad* pain or when a call to end a scene occurs, someone who will stand as a watchman over their sensual process, someone who cares.

If only these four steps were easy. Truthfully, they can be. However, we resist taking them for fear of leaving the fold, for fear of embracing a perspective that is different from most. Moreover, we resist taking these steps because of our attachment to the "way things are", the way we've become accustomed to reacting and behaving. There's comfort in familiarly, even if that familiarity doesn't serve our interests.

Still, there exists a possibility for a new way of being, a more masterful way of expressing your dominance and experiencing your rope bondage exchanges. A way through which, your sensual engagements will become understood and agreeable. Your desires will turn to choices, and you'll be received as a safe container for others to let go completely within.

As you follow this way, others will receive your awareness as dominance, the ease with which you express your skills as mastery and the connection you experience with your partner as control. But you'll know better, you'll know the truth. You'll know the way of a Zen rope master.

FINDING FREEDOM FROM PERFORMANCE ANXIETY

by Maria Shadoes

Like many other kinksters, I've spent a good deal of time debating how I came to have such early fantasies of bondage. Since I was 4 or 5 years old I fantasized about unseen machines forcing my body into a position where I could rub my genitals and holding me there. Suddenly it felt *really* good and then got boring. Bondage wasn't always involved, sometimes it was simply a power exchange where a powerful man or some sort of machine or institution forced me do it, sometimes by torture, sometimes by threats to my family. I have only come up with two viable answers... either my swaddling blankets were wrapped too tightly around me as an infant, or it's genetic.

As an adopted child I find the genetic theory more likely, having met my biological family seven years ago and finding the "Beauty Trilogy" on my momma's bookshelf and a "Spank Me" sticker on my sisters' mirror. In my adopted family there is no hint of understanding or tendencies in any of them, although there is love and tolerance in plenty. Since meeting my biological family I've done bondage photo shoots with my momma and with one of my sisters. Momma has even gone to Fetish Con and some other bondage events with me and modeled for a few other producers without me. Of course, this makes me believe the genetic theory for my own kink. Having heard similar stories from others allows me to think I'm not alone in being born kinky.

Being a tomboy, I spent a lot of time growing up with my older brother Dave's friends and I was good at being quiet when they started boasting about their sexual exploits as teenage boys often do. I learned a lot about how boys think. Looking back, I'm sure most of them probably didn't have much, if any, experience with girls. They were probably repeating what they'd heard their older siblings discussing and elaborating on that to make themselves seem more experienced and grown up. It was a lot of macho talk about how this girl was "dynamite in bed. She rode me like I was a wild stallion that she was trying to break" and another "sucked — and not in a good way! She just laid there; I might as well have been fucking a blow-up doll". This started my sexual performance anxiety. They seemed to complain more than they raved and I never wanted to be talked about in that negative way when I finally had sex with a guy.

Unfortunately, I never got real specifics on what they would have preferred — they probably didn't really know and only had their own fantasies to go on. While I had plenty of access to library books with clinical descriptions of sex, I certainly didn't have access to any porn movies or to books like the Kama Sutra or any books on how to improve your sex life. After all, I was too young to be thinking of having sex, or so everyone thought. I had been masturbating, and having orgasms since I was 4 or 5 years old though, so by the time I was 12 I had 7+ years of dreaming and fantasies that I desperately wanted to make come true.

Eventually I got a boyfriend who claimed to be experienced and I lost my virginity. I wanted an experienced man (but settled for a boy since I was still just a girl) because I felt that an experienced partner could guide me through the process. The soft, mushy love scenes in my historical romance novels bored me, and I dwelt endlessly on the scenes where the fair maiden was held captive and forced. I sought out boys who seemed naturally dominant and most likely to be like the heroes in those novels but it was a dismal failure. I'm ashamed to say that I was too scared to confess what I wanted to a guy. I think that I wanted them to just take me without being asked to and, of course, I was afraid they would tell me I was sick and needed psychiatric help if I told them I wanted to be tied up and play out force fantasy games.

So instead I spent years faking orgasms and getting excited each time I cast off an old boyfriend and got a new one hoping that this one would be *the one* who would just know what I wanted and do it. I couldn't seem to stop the cycle of faking orgasms because my boyfriends would be so hurt and desperate when I admitted to not reaching orgasm and I knew damn well that it was a mental block within me that only I could overcome. It seemed too cruel to let them try and try all the gentle, mushy stuff that they thought girls liked and it became a kind of torture for me.

I still liked the comfort and closeness that sex brought and I would just sneak off later, where I could put some rope around my neck (which I know now to be dangerous) and leave my pants around my ankles so that it felt like my legs were tied and wrap my undies around my wrists. Sometimes I just stuck my hands down my pants because they were so tight that it was self bondage of the quick and easy sort. I always reached orgasm by myself in well under 5 minutes, where a poor guy could spend hours trying with no results. Ahhhh — If only I'd been able to tell them to tie me up or at least hold me down!

And then there came Brian. Brian and I had been friends for 11 years before we started dating and our relationship coincided with me finding the internet and bondage boards. Brian loved to role-play and had he had a wonderful imagination. When I shyly told him about my interest in bondage he brought my fantasies to life. I finally orgasmed! A LOT. I would print out stories that I found on the internet and he would take the good parts from them and turn them into a "scene" with added Master/slave role play elements interwoven. I didn't know if I was really into BDSM at this point. I only wanted to be tied up, but everything that I read on the internet said that bondage is BDSM and if I liked it I'd like all sorts of other stuff too. It turned out to be true, but I'm still not sure that I believe that every person who wants to be tied up can be considered a BDSMer.

So, nervously we went to the Beyond The Edge Café, which was the only dungeon in Seattle at the time. We had dinner downstairs and watched another D/s couple where the man was feeding his bound partner and we loved it. We returned later for the play party, where we met a guy I had been talking to online who was going to flog me while Brian watched. The guy started giving me the pre-talk and when I turned around Brian had gone. He'd fled. I found him outside. He said that some of the bloody stuff was too much for him and that he had been hoping for a younger crowd and couldn't go back in there. Brian never went there with me again, but he had no problem with me going by myself so we continued that way for a couple of years. I went to play parties and played and learned and then came home and taught him as well as I could. He came up with some very intricate bondages for me. For a beginning rigger, what he did was actually quite amazing.

After Brian I somehow wound up with a local bullwhip expert for a couple of years. It gave me experience of a different type. Never enough bondage though. I never got enough bondage in all those years of playing in the scene, first solo and then with Rooster. He tried to suspend me once because I saw a suspension at the club and I wanted to do it so badly it made my teeth hurt. I couldn't breathe. I only lasted about 5 minutes and it was an agony of being unable to breathe. He tried to make adjustments and they only made it worse. I left that experience thinking that despite how badly I wanted it, my body just couldn't handle suspension.

Up until I started playing, I thought what I wanted was "comfortable bondage". When I met Lew Rubens and he did his first suspension on me, I knew otherwise. It hurt exquisitely, with sensations starting out as mere discomfort, but as time passed and rope was added that discomfort became mild pain, and then heavy pain and numbness... and then sublime subspace. I could never go back. Lew and I became almost inseparable soon after that first suspension even though it really turned our lives upside-down for awhile. I was in heaven. I got to experience being tied in ways I'd never even imagined. As soon as I recognized all the possibilities, I was quickly coming up with requests and suggestions for how I wanted to be tied. I stretched for a month and then came up with the straddled splits position that Lew figured out how to rig. That suspension tie, and some marketing by me, made us famous. Since then I look at everything to see how it could be used as a bondage prop and if it was designed as a bondage prop how I can use it differently than it's designer envisioned. Finding this niche and knowing it is where I belong has changed my whole outlook on life, my sex life was definitely altered for the better, and of course my career path changed as well. All of this from good bondage!

Now that I have explored so much bondage and found that I do indeed enjoy feeling helplessness and restraint along with my pain play and submission, I find myself looking back on listening to my brother and his friends. I was instilled with such performance anxiety, mostly about sex! I had fears of being a blow-up doll, or not being a wild stallion, or just not doing it right. But the truth is that when I'm tied up for sex I don't have to worry about any performance anxiety.

I was lucky enough to have nothing but bound sex for almost 5 yrs with Lew Rubens and it let me work a LOT of my internal issues out. Bondage as sexual anxiety treatment *can* work. Perhaps not for everyone, but it certainly did for me. Allow me to examine why. Let's face it, I'm usually gagged so kissing is a whole different experience, that eliminates the whole "I might have bad breath or be a bad kisser" issue. I don't have to worry about if I have any rhythm (I do not), since I can only move what they have allowed me or how they themselves move me, I don't have to wonder if the angle that works for my stimulation is boring for my partner, or if they want it fast when I want it slow.

I am now ever-so-much better at communicating with my partners and I can tell them what I like and what I don't. I don't have performance anxiety about sex anymore, having been with my current partner, Lee Chris, for a couple of years and talking freely with him and learning together how to please each other. Now that we know how to communicate openly, I find that I actually can orgasm without bondage on occasion and I'm actually enjoying experimenting with that, something that I once thought I'd never want again — unbound sex. I definitely don't want it that way all the time. Without actual bondage I'm still using bondage in my mind. It's mostly a matter of curiosity if I'll ever get to the point where I mostly don't use bondage at all to bring me to orgasm. Remembering my performance anxiety though makes me think that I cannot be the only person in the world who suffered from sexual performance anxiety and turned to bondage as a resolution.

As a top, I don't have sexual performance anxiety because I understand a submissive or bondage lover's mindset: that as long as I'm satisfied, and they are tied tightly and inescapably, a part of them is satisfied. Once again I'm freed from the worrying about whether my rhythm is wrong or my speed or angle off. I make a point to attempt to communicate with play partners so that I can learn how they are different from me as a bottom, and then adjust my style to accommodate their needs. But never to the complete sacrifice of my own needs. I know that I was never happy knowing someone was doing a scene exactly the way I wanted when it wasn't doing anything for them.

Part of the trick there is finding play partners I am compatible with. What I call "the kink within the kink". Some people are bondage lovers but only love bondage where they are left alone, or only with sexual stimulation or in contorted or only super comfortable positions. If I can't find scenes that both of us would enjoy then I figure perhaps they aren't the best play partner for me. I recommend TALKING first! I sure wish I could have heeded my own advice 20 years ago, but I had a mental block that wouldn't let words come out, even when the brain formulates exactly what they want to say.

Through hundreds of conversations trying to explain what I see in being tied up I have found that understanding a bondage bottom if you are not one yourself can sometimes be baffling and even frustrating for someone trying to please their bondage-loving partner. By considering the performance anxiety angle and trying things based on that, often wonderful experiences are the result. Here are some things I try to keep in mind.

- Using a gag eliminates anxieties they may have about having bad breath, bad teeth or just thinking they are bad kissers. When a gag is worn kissing can still be done but in some very erotic and imaginative ways that would otherwise not be done..

- Using a blindfold can eliminate stress caused by a partner who is self-conscious about you looking at them, or about watching you. I've seen both of these many, many times. If you are playing in public and they are distracted or made anxious by others a blindfold can also be helpful.

- Sometimes a bondage bottom is afflicted with poor self-esteem or pleasing their Top is what the scene is all about for them. If that is the case, I'm always sure to tell them often how attractive they look as the rope cuts into their flesh and how their suffering and the ability to use their bodies however I want is a huge turn-on for me. That is just in case they can't tell how erotic I find them by the way I'm rubbing my body all over theirs, assuming that sort of play is approved of and desired.

- Sometimes rope or other physical medium is not even a necessity for a good bondage scene. With a sexually submissive a stern command, with some form of repercussion that they will not like, to relax every muscle and lay completely still while you please yourself with their body is a wonderful bondage power exchange without rope. They will probably fail in this, but the first few times they move they will probably be testing the Top to see if they will truly do whatever it was they were threatened with — DO IT! I can almost guarantee they will be disappointed if you don't!

• I advocate talking about scenes afterwards, way afterwards, like the next day. Discuss what you each liked and didn't like about the scene and if you are both communicators you may be surprised at the insights that can be gained. As a talker myself, I ask them before a scene if they like to be talked to during a scene. If they do, saying things like "test your bonds so that you know you are truly, helplessly mine" working up to outlandish fantasy things that they may never admit to liking and may NEVER want to actually DO, but the thought will cause an instant orgasm. Things like, "I've invited a few friends over to watch tonight, I promised one that maybe you'd suck him/her off," or "I have a video camera here, we're making a porno tonight" (when they're blindfolded this works best). Myself — I find this very hot even though, on my checklist some of those things are hard limits.

• Make them THINK that you've left them alone. It can be quite stimulating for both of you if you mimic leaving but stay or peek through the keyhole. They will act more naturally and do what they really want to do when they think they are alone. Often what they want to do is simply lie still and enjoy the bondage.

The other form of performance anxiety that I deal with now is teaching and stage performances. I LOVE doing bondage and creating bondage art on human subjects. This has led to many opportunities to teach what I do and show it off. I remember when I first started doing photo shoots and making videos, I was terribly nervous and requested of the producer, Juliet Heart, that I be gagged as quickly as possible so I didn't have to try think of, or say, anything. Lew was worse than I was. He got so nervous he stuttered and sweated bullets. Back then I think I had the advantage. I was quickly tied up and, as I've said, once I'm tied up, there is no room for performance anxiety — of any kind. After a couple of dozen videos, both Lew and I were over our performance anxieties in front of the cameras. My being bound helped me to be over after the first 5 or 6 and I've found that it has easily transferred confidence to my Topping on camera as well.

I now tie all the time on camera and in videos without any performance anxiety, yet put me on a stage and sometimes I still yearn for the days when I was the one being tied up. Some of my best stage shows are self bondage and self suspension shows — it is the best of both of my loves. I think I will overcome my performance anxiety about teaching and stage shows the more I do it. My refusal to choreograph stage shows is probably slowing my confidence growth, but I so love to be spontaneous and go where the rope, the music and the person I'm tying all seem to lead me. I am seldom lucky enough to get a bottom who I've had a chance to rehearse with when I have been flown into an event. I often find out 5 minutes before a show that I can't do what I planned because she hurt her knee last night, or can't do inversions. I like being flexible and I'm hanging onto it stubbornly... and since it's hard to BE bound while I'm tying others (though not impossible), I'm still hanging on to a little bit of performance anxiety. I plan to start doing more where I am partially suspended, doing the suspensions and I'm guessing that with a bit of rope on me I will overcome this last performance anxiety.

I hope this glimpse into my world and what drives me to love bondage as my preferred form of BDSM play enlightens you in some small way about why we, or at least why *I* do the things we do. When I started boundtoloveit.com I had intended to do a lot of writing but I've not gotten to do nearly what I wanted to. I'm so glad that someone gave me the push I needed to sit down and write, to overcome this form of performance anxiety as well.

PERSONAL ROPE, UNIVERSAL POWER

by Mark Yu

"A human being results from the Qi of Heaven and Earth...
The union of Heaven and Earth is called human being"

Huang Ti Nei Ching Su Wen
(The Yellow Emperor's Classic of Internal Medicine)
Chapter, 25 First Published circa 100 BC

The quote above is from, *The Yellow Emperor's Classic of Internal Medicine.* It and a few other ancient texts are the foundation for the theories and practice of modern energetic medicine that has developed in Asia and around the world for the past 2 millennia. It is the basis for the theories used in Acupuncture, Tai Qi, Qi Gong, Kung Fu and many other healing and martial arts. It presents the idea that everything we are and experience is connected to the source of the entire Universe, and therefore, to each other in an intrinsic and fundamental way.

What does this, you may ask, have to do with the price of butt plugs in San Francisco? Well, more than you may think. I posit that this proven model of understanding and working with the Universal energy (Yin, Yang and Qi) for martial arts, healing, personal and spiritual development, is an invaluable tool and an essential component necessary for the growth and progression of all kinds of BDSM practice. I believe that this idea can be put to use to realize the unlimited potential that lies within all of us. This potential can be actualized in an especially efficient and effective way through the study and practice of a new style of Rope bondage and Power Exchange. Rope bondage has the special quality of being able to engage people on physical, mental and emotional levels. It is able to compress, bend, distort and engage people in a different and more complete way than many other techniques. To learn and implement these ideas, we must learn to see how Yin, Yang and Qi (pronounced "chee") move around and through us. We must learn to view our language, our motivation, our methods, our partners and most of all, **ourselves** in a **new way.** When we can see and understand our lifestyle and play in a context of a Universal system that touches each of us in a personal and intimate way, then the practice of our lifestyle becomes a vehicle for self development and mutual transformation. It can become a means to connect us to each other and to the source of Universal power. This is the true meaning of "Power Play."

One of the newest and more progressive trends in modern BDSM is the emergence of Rope (I will henceforth use the capitalized word "Rope" to mean all current rope trends including bondage, sensual play, decorative styles etc.) as a play style in itself. Though rope bondage has been around since rope was first used in the world, and since people began doing kinky things to each other, the trend in recent years has been one of rapid growth and diversity. Rope is being used in many ways by different types of people, both veterans to the lifestyle and new people who find it has an aesthetic and a feel that they can relate to. It has become popular with not only some people in the BDSM lifestyle, but also with artists, photographers, the adult entertainment industry and people who are just looking for something new to enhance their erotic life. Many find its utility and simplicity easy to work with and understand. Because of this rapid growth of interest in Rope, I think it's important to offer people a way to use it in a safe, constructive and progressive way.

The idea that Rope can be used in a way that is based on a Universal model of Qi similar to Oriental medicine and martial arts may seem strange to some but it is really very simple. Simple, and yet profound. In essence, this model says that all things (including people) are expressions of Yin, Yang and Qi. Yin and Yang is the force behind the tendencies of phenomena. The expression and movement of this phenomena is Qi. Qi may be considered as the manifestation of the interaction of Yin and Yang.

Now I know that some have heard things like, Yang is male and Yin is female, Yang is hard and Yin is soft and Yang is active and Yin is passive etc. These are partially, but not completely, true. The best way to understand this is, there is no "is" to Yin and Yang. The important thing to remember in learning to observe this in the world (and in our play) is that Yin and Yang are **not** specific qualities but are essentially different sides of the **same thing**. This model tells us that Yin and Yang are an expression of an opposition but also of inter-dependence. They both consume each other and yet support each other. It is an inter-transforming process that is inherent in all things. This model shows that Power Exchange is, in essence, the true nature of how the Universe functions. Now, THAT is what I call Power Play!

Here are some correspondences that may help us to see and understand the movement of Yin and Yang in our experience:

YANG	YIN
Active	Passive
Protective	Nutritive
Energy	Matter
Form	Substance
Execution	Planning

YANG	YIN
Hard	Soft
Outward	Inward
Wielding	Yielding

Examples of how Yin and Yang relate are infinite. But what is important to remember is that we do not fall into the trap of defining Yin and Yang as static qualities. Once we grasp the idea that Yin and Yang are two sides of the same thing and we are able to see them as a movement of energy or Qi, then we will begin to see its flow everywhere we look. We will become aware of how this interplay manifests and thus we will be able to have more insight into and more control over our Rope and Power Play.

To help understand how this applies to what we are talking about, let's look at a couple of examples from rope bondage and D/s.

Imagine you want to bind your partner. You ask your partner to fetch a rope from your bag. We may now consider your partner as Yang, in that they are moving to execute an action and are exerting an influence on something. Now, as anyone who uses rope knows all too well, it is very, pardon the term, limp. It is often difficult to keep rope in order. It flops and loops and tangles. This makes it very Yin. It has no real form for what we want to use it for.

You then take the rope, which we consider Yin, add your Qi, and in doing so transform it into Yang by tying a body harness on your now waiting, willing and patient partner. Your partner/bottom is now exhibiting the trains of being Yin by being receptive and quiet. The rope however, due to your input of Qi, can now be considered Yang in relation to your partner. It is giving form, Yang, to your partner, the substance, Yin. This shows the mutuality of Yin and Yang and how they change into each other. This changing is the manifestation and action of Qi.

In D/s, the examples are many, but let's take a simple one. Suppose you and your submissive enter a room with a large throne-like chair, perfect to exalt Your Glory! You sit and order your submissive to kneel before you and listen carefully. The submissive is now in a Yin, receptive state, open and waiting to be filled and given direction. You give your instructions with clarity and precision, Yang, as to how you would like to be served. You ask if they understand the instructions. You get an answer to the affirmative. You sit back and relax, Yin, and wait for them to be carried out, Yang. This interaction demonstrates how Qi transformed Yin into Yang and vice versa.

These examples are given to show the constant flux of Yin and Yang and how Qi permeates our actions and how important it is to observe and understand these Universal forces in our lives. These ideas are especially useful for those of us who live a lifestyle or play with Erotic Power Exchange, Rope and other BDSM activities. To help each other see, understand and relate in a new way, we need a common language that can give us a more precise way of communicating these ideas.

Language

In trying to comprehend the complex energies of people and the Universal forces that move and sustain them, acupuncturists and energetic physicians have developed a clear language that makes this daunting task easier. When gathering information about someone in order to make a diagnosis and develop a treatment plan, clear communication is of the utmost importance. Any misunderstanding can be problematic.

This is also very true of those who wish to practice Rope and Domination in a meaningful way. I find the current BDSM vernacular very inadequate for dealing with all the permutations of human experience that may arise while engaged in highly charged interactions. These interactions, that often involve many types of pain, emotional pressures, sexual situations, bodily stress and mental exertions, can have unknown and unwanted effects on those participating in them. If we are to be progressive in our lifestyle and interactions, we need to re-invent the language of BDSM and Power Play to fit the nuances and variations that naturally confront us. Instead of being an efficient language for the communication of complex human issues and experiences, the language that has been constructed uses quick labels that do not explore the sophisticated interplay involved in Rope and Power Exchange.

We must develop a language that is concise and yet able to facilitate the level of communication necessary to bring to fruition the full potential of how we interact. This is why I believe some feel the need to use the nebulous but somehow more accurate acronym, WIITWD. *What It Is That We Do.* We must ask our selves sincerely, "What is it that we are doing?" and perhaps more importantly, "Why are we doing it?"

Motivation

I, like most people, have different motivations when doing Rope. Sometimes I am motivated by a desire to dominate and manipulate a bottom's body for both mine and their pleasure. At times, I am even motivated to manipulate their minds and emotions as well as their body. At other times I do it to show others what I can do, or I do it behind closed doors as an expression of intimacy in private. All of these are valid on one level and in their own right. But what lies behind all of these is my primary and over-riding motivation, and that is to help my partner transform negative patterns into beneficial and healthy ones.

Whether that pattern is just a physical holding of a tight muscle group, an annoying mental thought process that is causing problems, a stubborn emotional blockage that is hindering harmonious living — or as is often the case a combination of all of these — my aim is to engage my partner in a way that no matter how rough or difficult the encounter is, they are left in a state that is better than when we began. This idea of transforming blockages and negative patterning is what a practitioner of Oriental Medicine has as their primary motive and we as practitioners of a new way of doing Rope and Domination should also have as the force behind our actions. These forces that shape our motives are critical for us to understand.

The only way we can begin to see the patterns of another human being in a clear and unhindered fashion is to work on developing our capacity for seeing ourselves. This practice of setting a priority on self-observation is the first step to seeing others clearly. If this priority is integrated into our motives and actions, the possibilities are endless. If we are able to see ourselves as we ourselves act, we are then able to wield formidable power or yield to it in a way that better allows a creative application of Qi and the wonderful sensations and transformation that can follow. This in turn will make our immersion in kinky, sexual and extreme behavior a meaningful, healing and positive force.

Motivation is the raw force behind Intention. Intention is the focus for our motivation. It allows us to give form, Yang, to every interaction we fully engage in. If motivation is why we do things, then intention is what we will do. Intention is very important to keep direction and control over during our interactions in Rope. To know what we intend is to begin to create it. There has been much discussion about this by many influential people in the BDSM community for good reason. However, it is only half of what it takes to make Rope and Domination meaningful and productive.

The other essential part is Awareness. Having an awareness of the things around you, of your partner, and of your self is critical to exerting power and control over your partner and achieving your aim with your Rope and with your expression of Power Play. Taking in your situation and being open, Yin, is what gives us the information we need to make our interaction more satisfying and meaningful. Many have intentions of all sorts, but not all have the awareness to see how, why or if what they intend to do is appropriate, safe and relevant to the situation at hand. We need to realize, the more aware we are in any situation, the more we are able to manifest our intention. I believe this idea needs much more emphasis in BDSM education, training and practice. With a focused intention and an active awareness, we are truly able to explore our selves, our relationships and are able to bring a healing transformation to those we interact with. We must learn to place a high value and priority on our internal orientation and where we place our attention. When we are able to do this, it becomes possible to make our Rope and Domination a pathway to intimate self expression, artistic endeavor, technical accomplishment and mutual healing and growth. Not to mention making it damn satisfying too!

Method

When we have become familiar with a Universal model, have come to a consensus on a working vocabulary, and we have begun to understand our motivations — the next step is applying a proven method. Our method must help us to understand who we are interacting with and why, and it must give us an efficient means to carry out our intention in the proper context of communication and action.

In Rope and Domination, we have a special tool. Because of how adaptable rope is to almost any situation, it is a wonderful way to engage and connect with our partners and express our Power Play to its utmost. But before we can use it properly, we must lay a foundation of basic knowledge and competence.

It is fundamentally important for every practitioner of Rope to have a solid foundation in basic skills. These include but are not limited to: learning how bodies are built and function, knowing how to assess a partner for potential problems and benefits, mastering proper rope technique and safety, and of course, having a developed and focused intention and awareness. Without these as a foundation, there is very little that can be done on anything other than a most basic level. Luckily for the Rope practitioner, there are many resources and opportunities for learning these skills. It is the humble seeker of knowledge of their art that reaps the rewards of its blessings. Those who wish to know more about their art and themselves are those who will be able to grow and create and will define how the art of Rope progresses.

When the Rope practitioner has a good grasp of the basics and has found a solid center inside themselves, they are able to add other more powerful elements to their practice such as breath, pain, eroticization, protocols and rituals. As a practitioner of Rope and Domination progresses and grows, using more and more complex elements, they will have an opportunity to expand their influence and power on their chosen path and make their relationships and personal expression of their chosen lifestyle strong and healthy.

"In order to weaken, it is necessary first to strengthen,
In order to destroy, it is necessary first to promote,
In order to grasp, it is necessary first to give."

Chap. 36, Tao Te Ching
Lao Tzu, a Wise Dominant from the 7th Century BC

The above quote, from the classic Taoist work by Lao Tzu, gives us an excellent example the concept of Yin and Yang and how we must learn to apply it in a modern Rope and Power Exchange context. The inter-action and mutual support of energy, emotions, sensations, and experiences through a connection forged with attention, caring and skill is what Power Exchange is truly all about. The quote above tells us that to make Power Play work and have meaning, it must never become static. To exert power, we must first yield to the other side of it in some way. This allows us to not only understand how to manifest our desires, but actually allows it to come to pass more efficiently and with very little effort. Whether we are receiving or giving service, doing forceful rope domination with takedowns and capture scenarios or executing an elaborate ritual involving a high level of protocol, this idea of giving a bit of one thing to get the opposite is a Universal principle and a wise way to align ourselves with the laws of how the universe works.

When we are able to use our personal Rope style in a way that makes use of these Universal forces, we are able to ride a wave of infinite power and endless variety. We can achieve an ever higher level of awareness of ourselves and our partner and are able to control our focus on what we want and need. We will have raised our consciousness enough to become a creative power in our own right. This state of being gives us the ability to merge with others, exchange unlimited power and share countless variety of sensations and experiences via a connection more profound than our ordinary state of being, but as easily accessible as a coil of rope in our bag. All we have to do is want it enough to reach out for it, take it and share it.

MATCHING INTENTIONS — FINDING THE RIGHT PARTNER

by LadyGold

So I'm a submissive and you are a Dom; that means we will fall in love, ride off into the sunset and live happily ever after — right? Well, not exactly. I think we all know that people are different and in "the lifestyle" we are used to negotiating limits. And so people ask, "Do you like bondage?" But seldom do they ask — "Why do you like it?" For the past several years, I've been presenting a workshop on the Psychology of Bondage — Not How To — but Why To. I got the idea for it because I discovered that I personally needed a certain emotional environment — an *intent* — for bondage to be enjoyable and that not every partner had the same idea. Over time I've collected a variety of types or styles of bondage — each with a different intent.

Bondage by definition includes giving over control on the part of the submissive/ bottom and taking control by the Dominant/Top. But it's where the scene goes after that exchange has taken place that can make the scene enjoyable — or if not enjoyable at least fulfilling instead of a negative experience.

Here's a description of the experience that started my interest in intent. I agreed to be tied up by a well known bondage artist and educator. He put me into a very restrictive hog tie and then said, "OK — let's see you get out of that!" (insert evil cackle). He actually had someone timing me and I managed to get loose in 13 minutes and 26 seconds. He asked me if I'd agree to a second tie and I agreed. He had watched what I did to get loose the first time and the second time he made some adjustments to his rig that prevented my escaping. I struggled for a considerable amount of time and then gave up. I safeworded, "Beige — for boredom". He was delighted; he had restrained me; he had come up with an inescapable tie. But the experience was not fun for me and I wouldn't have repeated it. Once I found I could not escape, the "game" was over for me. Our intents were not the same. In this case no harm was done since neither of us was looking at the scene as anything other than a rather lighthearted event. But if we had been considering each other as potential long term partners it could have been very disappointing.

My then significant other and I were teaching and doing suspension bondage; and I found that to be a very rewarding experience. So what was the difference? We were working together towards a common goal; it was not a case of his trying to impose his will on me. In a very real sense we were working on an engineering project together. I wasn't expected to try to escape; in fact I was needed to not escape; to be a willing participant. We communicated throughout the process; we cooperated. Our intents were very much aligned. He still was in control; he tied the ropes and placed my body but overall we functioned as partners.

Another submissive in the first instance might have been delighted to have it demonstrated that the hog tie was inescapable and not feel the slightest bit of interest in providing feedback during a suspension. It's (you guessed it) all a matter of intent.

Once I realized how important intent or headspace was in a scene and in a continuing relationship, I began looking for other instances. And a few weeks later I had the opportunity of being involved with two other couples at an out of town event. One couple consisted of an extremely attractive woman wearing thigh high stockings, six inch heels and a skirt that barely covered... well much at all. Where my S.O. and I use sturdy natural fiber ropes like hemp or jute, this Dom was using white nylon and creating what was clearly a damsel in distress as popularized by Bettie Paige or such as graced the covers of 1940s detective magazines. As I chatted with them afterwards I realized they hadn't discussed intent but that he thought of himself as an artist and her as his canvas; for her part she was delighted to be turned into a cover girl and admired for her beauty. Inescapability was not a factor nor was she expected to have any input into the process. I would have found myself bored (again) and not many Doms would have the patience to make each turn of rope just so… but it suited them. Their intents were very nicely aligned.

If you have ever watched Shibari being done you've likely seen another sort of artist. In Shibari there are very specific places to put the strands of rope and names like Ebi, Karada or Takakote to describe the particular rig. Again everything has to be just so; but it is the ropework that requires the artistry. For this reason (and to get a laugh at my workshops) I describe the Bettie Paige style as a "pretty girl and a rope" and Shibari as "pretty rope and a girl." In both cases, the Dom/Top/Rigger is the artist and the sub/bottom is just the platform for the artistry. Those of us (cough) who identify as "attention sluts" generally enjoy these types of scenes.

So I guess it's time to talk about sex, eh? Clearly not all bondage involves sex but for many of us it is at least an adjunct. Restraint allows a certain degree of plausible deniability; "I couldn't help myself — he had me all tied up". Restraint also allows our inner animals a chance to come out. I've found this to be particularly true in case of female Doms and male submissives. Guys just don't want to accidentally hurt their Doms so they don't think they can fight back. Well placed ropes allow them the ability to struggle without worrying about harming their partners. Early on I heard the phrase, "When the ropes go on the outside — they come off the inside." and I've found this to be very true. Many inhibitions can be released when it's clear that there are definite boundaries.

Struggling is not always what the bottom enjoys though. A good many of the submissives in my workshops identify with the idea of "bondage as security". Many feel that tight, restrictive bondage is like a full body hug. It's comforting and protective. Some even go as far as full mummification. It's worth mentioning here that that sort of scene is not for beginners, but that sensory deprivation can represent the ultimate submission as well as a chance for the submissive to go on a very personal inner journey.

At the other end of the spectrum from these sensual types of bondage are those involving pain, punishment and predicament bondage. These are all types which to a greater or lesser degree are inflicted by the Dominant on the submissive. Because of the possibility of real harm — not only physically but also emotionally — to the submissive, this sort of scene must be negotiated with the submissive and the intent of the participants must be very clear.

By its very nature bondage can be painful at times and in the classic sadist/ masochist relationship it is a virtual staple. But as I hope I've made clear there are far more styles or types than just S and M. So how do you determine what sort of submissive/bottom you are dealing with? And is there a way to be sure that the scenes are fulfilling to both of you?

I've looked at the strictly mental aspects of bondage — the headspace involved, and discovered six broad categories:

- Submission

- Loss of Control

- Gear Fetish

- Endorphins

- Fear/Intensity

- Just Plain Bondage

Submission

A slave or submissive is generally interested in bondage only because it is something their Dom/Top/Master is doing to them. The type of bondage is unimportant so long as they can demonstrate their submission; their main focus is in the relationship to their partner. At times merely telling a submissive not to move is as good as spending 30 minutes on a complicated Shibari harness.

Loss of Control

Someone who wishes to lose control is oftentimes confused with a submissive but, in fact, they are not necessarily submitting to their partner as much as they are submitting to the bondage itself. They want to feel helpless and the Dom is only providing that opportunity to them. These bottoms may find cages or mummification most attractive.

Gear Fetish

The Gear Fetishist has specific interests; chains versus rope or leather cuffs versus metal ones. It is the equipment itself that provides the turn on. Many times they even already own what they find attractive. A straight jacket, for example, or a full rubber body suit.

Endorphins

Those who are endorphin junkies are generally what we think of as true masochists. They enjoy not the pain itself but the endorphins the body creates in response to pain. Often referred to as a "runner's high", these endorphins produce a state of mind or euphoria which masks the pain. In their case, bondage may just be a way to restrain them so that the whipping/flogging can take place.

Fear/Intensity

Fear and intensity lovers need to be taken out of their everyday mind set. They are looking for adrenalin though, not endorphins. They crave danger and arousal. I put myself in this category because I have a fear of falling and yet I enjoy being suspended. I may shriek when the ropes slip just a bit — but I want to do it again!

Just Plain Bondage

Finally there are those bottoms that just plain enjoy bondage. They aren't particularly into submitting or interested in losing control; they aren't after endorphins or adrenalin and it doesn't much matter what you use on them to retrain them... so long as you do restrain them. In this group are the folks that enjoy self-bondage as much as with a partner.

I've also noticed that in some case bondage becomes the coin of the realm; i.e., it becomes something that can be traded for another activity — barter if you will. I think so long as both parties are aware that this is a trade (I'll tie you up if you'll have sex with me) it can be a fulfilling exchange. But there is the potential for dishonesty so clarity of intent is (again) very important.

As with everything else involved in what it is that we do, not everyone is one particular type forever and always. Speaking for myself although I enjoy an adrenalin rush, I also very much enjoy just submitting to my partner and when he isn't interested in pushing my limits, I'm quite content to curl up next to him in my collar and chains. Although I used to claim to be purely submissive, I discovered while helping out at bondage workshops that I very much enjoy being a rigger myself and so I've begun to call myself a submissive rope Top. I do macramé; it just happens to have people inside.

There are probably at least as many reasons for wanting to tie up your partner as there are for wanting to be tied. I think the most classic example is the Dominant who simply wants to be in control and uses bondage to demonstrate that. The Dominant I described at the beginning of this article fits that description. In other cases, the Dominant enjoys inflicting pain, or pleasure or inducing a reaction such as fear. Bondage can be used in all these situations to "force" the submissive to endure what the Dom wishes to inflict. The artistic Dominant wants a canvas. The Fetishist Dom wants someone to share his/her love for rubber, leather or what have you.

So how do you go about figuring out what sort of person you are dealing with? If you just ask something like, "So tell me what you like about bondage." You may not get very far with an inexperienced bottom although you may get some very specific answers from someone who has been the in the scene for a while. I've discovered in my workshops though that many folks may not be very self aware but by the time I finish the workshop they are ready to go out and try something they've never done because now that they know about it... it's hot.

Try some general questions like "How did you get interested in the scene?" If they tell you they went to Rubber Night at the local group — you've found a Gear Fetishist. Or if you notice they call you Ma'am or Sir automatically they are probably submissive. Do they like to ride roller coasters when they go to an amusement park? They're likely to be an adrenalin junkie. Don't be afraid to ask them what attracted them to you. If it's the flogger you have hanging on your belt they well may be a masochist looking for endorphins.

Ask them what sort of scenes they have most enjoyed — even if they don't include bondage. If they watch or read porn — what have they seen or read that turns them on? It's been my experience that men watch porn and women read it. But it's way beyond the scope of this article to speculate on why that is the case.

Probably the most telling question is "What do you fantasize about when you masturbate?" This is especially useful with newbies who really don't know what is possible — just what turns them on.

It isn't necessary for your intents to be an exact match. A Fetishist Dom may find that an intensity/fear bottom enjoys wearing a gas mask — not as gear but as something that gives them an adrenalin rush. The Dom who enjoys inflicting pleasure often matches well with a submissive who needs to be tied up in order to feel out of control. The Artistic Dom is a fine match for the submissive who just enjoys bondage — period.

This article isn't designed to be a How To — but rather a Why To, so I'll leave it to your imagination to figure out What to Do — after you've figured out the sort of bottom you are dealing with. Hopefully by now, though you have some idea of Who To. Mostly it boils down to being aware of what you (bottom or Top) want out of the scene and making sure that your partner has, if not the same, at least a compatible intent. To that end, communicate, communicate, communicate! And, as I end each of my workshops, remember:

There is No One True Way.

MAGICK, SPIRITUALITY, AND PARADOX IN ROPE BONDAGE

by Ariana Dawnhawk and Ryan

Thus bind thyself, and thou shalt be for ever free.[2]

When Aleister Crowley penned these words circa 1910, he certainly wasn't talking about rope bondage. But this piece of wisdom is no less applicable. It eloquently expresses the paradox of rope bondage, and magick thrives on paradox. With bondage comes freedom.

Our spirituality is heavily influenced by both witchcraft and ceremonial magick. Our sex life and our spirituality feed each other in a delicious symbiotic relationship. We find that kink in its many forms works well with sex magick, and rope bondage was our first foray into kink.

Rope bondage reflects the same paradox that begins this essay. On the surface, D/s looks like one person taking power over another, and rope bondage viscerally represents this. How can one who is bound truly be free? A skilled rigger can tie a bottom such

---

2 Aleister Crowley, "Liber III vel Jugorum"

that escape is impossible. The bottom is, on the physical plane, powerless. The bottom could be raped, dismembered, or killed, without even a fighting chance.

A common perception of bondage, in the myths that shape the spirituality of many cultures, is that of punishment. Prometheus brought about the ire of the Gods, and He was tied to a rock and tormented by birds picking out his liver. But this punishment occurred due to an act of empowerment; Prometheus brought the skill of fire to humans. Power is woven into the mythos, often in complex ways. Several Gods have stepped into their power by choosing to submit through the power exchange inherent in bondage or suspension.

In Norse mythology, Odin and the Æsir feared the great wolf Fenrir, child of Loki, due to a prophecy that He would kill Odin at Ragnarok. So They challenged Fenrir to a contest of bondage. Fenrir agreed to be bound with the chain named Leyding, from which he escaped easily. Fenrir agreed to a greater challenge, and the Æsir bound Him with the chain Dromi, from which Fenrir also escaped, but with difficulty. Odin, greatly troubled by Fenrir's strength, had dwarves create a magic ribbon, named Gleipnir. Fenrir, suspecting trickery, demanded surety that He would be released if He were unable to escape, and Tyr agreed to place His hand in Fenrir's mouth. After much struggling, Fenrir found that He could not escape, and the Æsir had no intention of releasing Him, so Fenrir bit off Tyr's hand. The Æsir then bound Fenrir to a stone and drove a sword through His jaw. This, being one of the earliest recorded examples of Dominants ignoring safewords, also spelled the doom for Odin; for Fenrir eventually did escape at Ragnarok, killing Odin for his trickery.

The Sumerian Goddess Inanna chose to abandon Her temples to descend to the underworld. She divested all Her jewelry and clothing, symbolizing Her power, identity, and Godhood, to enter the underworld, only to be judged, struck dead, and suspended from a hook. Like Fenrir, Inanna must have suspected what awaited Her, for she had made prior arrangements with Her minister Ninshubur, who pleaded with the Gods for help when She did not return for three days. Enki sent a rescue party later and resurrected Her from the dead. She truly stepped into Her power as a Goddess, becoming an awesome force, and Her vengeance extended to Her husband Dumuzi. For failing to mourn Her, She condemned Him to live in the underworld for six months out of the year.

The story of Inanna predates a pivotal event in the mythology of another religion by a good three to four thousand years. A man born miraculously from a virgin became unpopular with the Roman government. Rather than tell them what they wanted to hear, He chose submission in the form of flogging and suspension to a cross by ropes and nails, resulting in His death. Like Inanna, He resurrected three days later in glory. Nearly two thousand years later, this event is still widely celebrated.

Fenrir, Inanna, and Jesus all chose submission through bondage in its most extreme forms, suspecting or knowing what awaited them. Had They not done so, They likely would be little more than footnotes in the history of religion. And yet Their submission brought each of Them into power and divinity. The restriction of bondage, paradoxically, can be one of the most empowering acts. Thus they bound themselves, and became forever free.

This paradox of rope bondage becomes evident in orgasm. For us, orgasm can be a moment of touching the limitless and connecting to the All, as well as each other. Sexual climax is one of the most accessible ways of feeling truly free. And, paradoxically, submitting to bondage can enhance this freedom. We find that the intensity of orgasmic expansion is increased as we feel the restriction of the ropes, which leads to even greater expansion. We both savor the feeling of coming while straining against ropes biting into our flesh.

When asked if we're tops, bottoms, or switches, we identify instead as rheostats. Switches have two positions — the polarized ends of a scale. A rheostat, or dimmer switch, has quite a lot of territory in between the extremes. We do polarized scenes sometimes, with intense D/s headspace. We may also tie each other decoratively for a scene, or take turns tying each other up, or tie harnesses on each other and then bind them together. Many of our scenes aren't D/s, and sometimes we blur the distinction between top and bottom.

All of the magickal paths we practice contain threads of stepping into and standing in one's power. For us, power is flexible, flowing and changing but always present. Submitting and dominating are both expressions of power, and we think it is necessary for someone to be grounded in their own power to have D/s flow in its full capacity.

Choosing to submit or to dominate holds tremendous power, embodying paradox. Both choices can be acts of Will. Crowley's definition of magic as "the art and science of causing change in conformity to Will" makes this act magical. Rope, like many ritual tools, physically and symbolically marks this change. Combining rope with the energy raised by sex can lead to very powerful magic indeed.

When we first experimented with kink and heavy D/s headspace in scene, it flowed very well, almost too well. This scared Ari, and she wasn't sure these were good things that worked with the rest of her life and path. In spite of this, she suggested going to an evening rope workshop, and afterwards expressed interest in driving over five hundred miles to attend a weekend rope bondage intensive. The whole time, she was saying she wasn't sure she'd ever want to do anything kinky again. There was a disconnection; something wasn't flowing right.

After the first rope workshop, we talked about kink for a long time. At one point, as Ari was calming down, beginning to realize that she really did love BDSM and that this was okay, Ryan saw her struggling with desire and fear. He had an idea. He felt that an immediate rope scene could be a magical act that could help her integrate this. So he told Ari that he wanted to tie her, right then and there. This was an edgy request as we generally keep clear boundaries to our scenes; we had never previously pulled the other into scene without discussion and advance warning. Ari didn't say anything, but she was thinking that it would be okay. Ryan began.

Ryan bound Ari's hands quickly, using them to pin her to the bed, kissing her hard. Then he tied her ankles together with her legs crossed. He attached a rope to the ankle ties and wrapped it over one shoulder, under the other, back to her legs, and doubled the rope back again over the opposite shoulder. This pulled her body forward, and when he tied the rope off, he rolled her onto her back, leaving her pleasantly exposed and very vulnerable. It was a tie we had just learned, and Ryan chose this because Ari had volunteered to demonstrate this at the workshop in front of a room full of people. This was further proof that doing rope bondage was her Will, in spite of her denial. He said a mantra over and over, "You are safe. You are powerful. This does not run sideways" as he pulled her around, pulled her hair, scratched her, and spanked her. We had sex with Ari tied like this, both of us reaching orgasm as Ryan recited the mantra. Ari cried a little during the scene — not because of pain or sadness, but because this cathartic experience had opened her up.

And it worked. Ari knew in her bones that kink truly worked for her, and although issues have occasionally surfaced, overall she is much more comfortable with kink and knows how important it is to her. Since then, she thinks about the scene and how it felt whenever issues arise, and it reminds her that all this does run true. In this scene, tying her up was a way of making space for her to unbind something in herself and open the way for herself. Since then, we've associated the Egyptian God Wepwawet, the Opener of Ways (and a deity to whom we are both deeply devoted) with kink and honored Him in this context.

In doing the work of Wepwawet, we seek to open the way for others to facilitate transformation. This does not mean changing another person. Rather, it is like opening a door; the other person can choose to walk through it as an act of will, or can take a different path. It reminds us of another favorite quote from Crowley:

But as to each man that keeps his true course, the more firmly he acts, the less likely others are to get in his way. His example will help them to find their own paths and pursue them. Every man that becomes a Magician helps others to do likewise.[3]

We also enjoy using rope in a decorative context. Part of our work has involved sacred adornment and reclaiming beauty from how it has been twisted and turned into a commodity. Rope is a flexible tool, and interesting, paradoxical energy flows through using something that could so easily restrict to beautify instead, or to do both at once. Knowing one's own beauty and making a space for someone to realize theirs is also dangerous. Touching this edge, we honor Melek Ta'us, the Peacock Angel, as we were introduced to Him in the Feri Tradition, an American flavor of witchcraft emphasizing ecstatic worship. He is beauty and power and danger, the Lover and Opposer held under the hand of love, and we, as well as several other Feri practitioners we know, strongly associate Him with kink.

It is widely believed that Japanese rope bondage began as a means to detain prisoners. This military aspect connects well with several of our spiritual paths. Victor Anderson, founder of the Feri tradition, referred to Feri practice as a martial art. T. Thorn Coyle, an initiate of the Feri tradition, works with the ethic of the Warrior using a pentacle with five points: Commitment, Honor, Truth, Strength, and Compassion, flowing back to Commitment. We find that this pentacle applies very well to kink and power exchange.

---

3 Aleister Crowley, "Magick in Theory and Practice"

Commitment represents the covenants made between Dominant and submissive regarding their roles and their limits, one's Commitments to oneself, and the shared Commitment to engage in the scene. Honor signifies the value, pride, and respect one places in one's role as a Dominant or as a submissive. Truth represents one's self-knowledge, as well as the awareness and the gnosis that one experiences during the scene. Strength is the power that carries both the Dominant and the submissive through the scene. Compassion runs towards both self and other. Each person needs Compassion for self, realizing one's own boundaries. It runs through the Dominant as care and protection of the submissive who has exchanged so much power; this Compassion is not at all incompatible with making severe the ordeals. And the submissive serves the Dominant with compassion. Each upraises the other. Good after-care is another means of Compassion. (Yes, Dominants need after-care, too!) And this Compassion builds the connection between the two partners, strengthening the Commitment for further play.

War dieties, we find, make good allies in rope bondage. Wepwawet marches before the Pharaoh's army, quite literally opening the way. Ari has also honored Aphrodite in a kink context, both as the Lady of love and beauty and in her fiercer aspects, such as Summakhia, Ally in War. Ryan also works with Scáthach, a female warrior in Irish mythology who trained the warrior Cúchulainn. Scáthach first came to Ryan quite literally by challenging him in battle, encouraging him to fight harder in a martial arts class drill. We both associate Scáthach as having a particular strength through flow state.

When Ryan was having difficulty with submission, finding himself able to submit physically to bondage and pain but mentally and emotionally resisting, we both did magickal work with Scáthach. Ari, who also honors Scáthach, left an obsidian blade on Scáthach's shrine to charge with Her energy. Ryan called upon his connection to Her as Ari bound Ryan with ropes and blindfolded him. She alternated between striking him and caressing him with a cloth; each time Ryan found himself mentally resisting or bracing against the scene, he called on Scáthach to help him relax into sub-space. Ryan had no warning that any knife play would occur until he caught the unmistakable smell of isopropyl alcohol. And when the blade sliced repeatedly into his skin, he felt as if he were being flayed alive, thought he might need stitches, and yet he was so far gone into sub-space that it didn't even matter. Ari then rode him, tied and bleeding, to mutual orgasm. Ryan did not, in fact, need stitches; a blindfold can make a dull butter knife feel like a scalpel. And several months later, when we both had the courage to take off our clothing and have a mutually fierce rope bondage scene at our first play party, we left our orange paper wristbands bearing the dungeon's name on Scáthach's shrine as an offering and as an acknowledgment. They have stayed there ever since.

Another deity we honor in a BDSM context is Set, the opposer and challenger in the Egyptian pantheon. Set is greatly misunderstood — he is the god of the outsider and the Other, the necessary chaos that is a part of existence, and that which strengthens by contending.

To the majority of people, rope and other aspects of kink is "other." Even to kinky people, there can be an aspect of taboo and transgression. This places kink firmly in Set's domain. The energy of transgression can be applied to spellwork, as well.

Shortly after moving in with Ryan, Ari was in a car accident. Luckily, the only injuries were to the vehicles involved, and her car was fairly heavily damaged. Ari wanted it repaired, or at least wanted a fair insurance settlement for it if it were totaled.

We both felt we should do sex magic to charge a sigil for this intent. Ari had previously named her car Serenity, so we used a pendant that said "Serenity" in Chinese characters as our sigil. To raise more energy through transgression, and to intensify orgasm through the feeling of constriction, we decided that Ari would be tied when she came. Ari held the pendant on her chest, and throughout the scene both of us concentrated on the pendant, funneling the energy of our orgasms towards the sigil represented by the pendant, which channeled the energy toward our desired outcome. While Ari's car did end up being totaled, she certainly received a fair settlement.

Working with power, transgression, and unbinding can bring many issues to the surface. Various witchcraft traditions and other spiritual and magical paths have borrowed Jung's concept of the Shadow, the parts of the self that one considers unpleasant or unacceptable and buries. When Shadow isn't acknowledged, the power of Shadow can insidiously run sideways, causing harm in ways that may be difficult to identify. We feel that to be whole, one needs to acknowledge and integrate one's Shadow.

Bondage and D/s are ways to play with the Shadow, acknowledging issues around power and making them physical and sexy. In the context of a scene, or in choosing a D/s relationship, the paradoxes of hierarchy and control are explicitly acknowledged and not pushed aside to surface in unhealthy ways. BDSM gives people the opportunity to dialogue with sex and power in accordance with Will, and can further the magic of making their lives.

ANATOMY OF A SCENE

by Tony Buff and Derek da Silva

Bondage has primacy in the realm of BDSM. Not because it is the first letter in some acronym (although perhaps that says something too), but rather that, for many of us, it is the first kink play we engage in and it forms the base on which many scenes are built. Bondage can be as easy as child's play, but it evolves with its practitioners, and it can become extremely advanced and challenging for top and bottom alike. Whether expanding the limits of an experienced player or introducing a novice to their personal understanding of the power exchange, bondage plays a major role. For many of us, our first kink experiences are bondage. Bondage is practiced widely and is deeply ingrained in our cultural memory.

> **Derek:** I used to tie myself up with life preserver straps as a very young child. Later as kids we'd take turns playing Harry Houdini by tying each other up to see who could escape fastest. As innocent as this play seems, it was motivated by the same erotic dynamic of power and control that many of us enjoy as adults.

> **Tony:** I remember tying myself up with rope, cutting my clothes off with knives and playing out abduction fantasies in my head before I even reached adolescence. Perhaps these deep seeded inclinations were sparked by images of Robert Conrad as James T. West bound

shirtless in the Wild Wild West. Looking back, it must have been good preparation for my initiation into my first S/m family, which included being hog-tied, dumped in a muddy back yard and left in the rain for hours. Adding water to hemp is one sure way to delay escape, 'cause that shit shrinks!

Bondage can take many forms. It can be as subtle as a verbal order to stay in place, perhaps with an indicator to show when the sub has violated this order. Or it can involve elaborate contraptions of metal and steel, boxes and cages, and even novel control points like needles and sutures. And of course there is that old standby, rope. For us, it is hemp rope that holds the deepest, most primal magic.

What these forms share in common is a means of enforcement of control over the bottom's physical movement. For some of us, the mere thought of one person placing another in bondage is filled with erotic undertones. Taking control away or giving it up is an exquisite act of intimacy. In a world of sexual play based on power, bondage is control in its most direct form. As such, it is a great way to create and enforce power relationships in a scene. It is also a way to make many intense scenes safer by limiting a bottom's ability to thrash and inadvertently cause injury. By allowing himself to be bound, the sub submits to the control of the top. This is a powerful and liberating experience. By giving up control, you have permission to explore places you might not otherwise visit. Bondage can focus the mind, support the body, or free the spirit.

This paradox of bondage as freedom has many dimensions. A straight guy might allow himself to be tied up in order to be freed from social restrictions. A rather service oriented sub, intent on following orders, can enjoy struggling. In predicament bondage, a Dom can give the sub just enough freedom to choose between different unattractive options, creating tension and struggle.

And in advanced BDSM scenes bondage can be a prime tool, acting as a safety net against real injury even as it facilitates expanding limits and consent to their edge. But the reason bondage is so important to us is that it acts as a ritual to radically transform the headspace in which a scene occurs.

We've both worked with many different materials for bondage. Nylon is soft and glides easily. This makes it attractive when you are first learning since it's soft on the bottom and easy for the top to work with. Cotton has it own attractions in that it has more "tooth" and thus any knots hold up better under a struggle. We've also done bondage with some pretty unusual materials.

> **Tony:** When I started topping, I created a rope kit of multi-fiber cordage with similar properties to nylon. There were different colors for the different lengths and all the ends were sealed with tool dip. As my rigging matured however, so did my choice in rope. The multi-fiber cord was left in its bag for years until I needed it for a workshop or demo. When the boy that was assisting me saw the rope he made a bee-line for the bright colors. "What pretty rope. Why haven't we used this before," he asks as he reaches out to feel the lengths, then with complete understanding, "Oh, pillow rope."

> **Derek:** Once I did a full Shibari hogtie using a long orange extension cord — because Shibari rarely uses knots, this actually wasn't so difficult.

> **Tony:** Derek had me suspend him in a web of bungee cords — this was great because he could pull and thrash, but the cords always sprang him back into position.

Still it is hemp we love the best...

Raw and organic, hemp involves all the senses. Its texture is rough and unyielding, while hiding a certain softness. Its weight makes a satisfying thud as it hits the deck, and it almost hums as it is pulled against itself. Its smell is intense and used as a gag it has a taste that is earthy. Visually beautiful, the wild origin of its material plays against the rigid order of its twisted strands. A master rigger's rope flows like chi and becomes an extension of them in a way that leather fetters or steel chains are hard pressed to match. The rope runs over the submissive's body and becomes part of a ritual that is as unique as each individual and situation. It can seduce submission, structure play, and frame an entire scene.

Rope play is the foundation for a good majority of our scenes. The acts of binding and unbinding the ropes are like bookends to the scene, bringing us into and back out of an altered state of consciousness where each of us goes deep into our mindsets of Dom and sub. While we may live a 24/7 Dom/sub lifestyle, it's in the special moments of BDSM play where these roles are lived most deeply.

Derek: When Tony makes his first wraps of rope across my body I instantly have a deep physical response in the pit of my stomach that becomes an intense sense of submission and sexual excitement. Tony's rope makes me hard instantly. As he lays more rope on and the bindings get tighter and more restrictive I fall trance-like into my headspace. Here I am free and no longer need to run the show. I am in trusted hands, and within these bounds all my sensations, all the responses are permitted.

Tony: For me, running the rope allows me to connect more deeply with my boy, to take control over every inch of his body, and focus my mind in the meditation of rope and control. Likewise, after a heavy scene, a gradual and sensual removal of my work helps me reconnect with the boy, and carefully take him back to the real world. Re-coiling the rope with care, acts as a final act that brings us back and reestablishes order.

Rope bondage can also be a scene onto itself. Ornamental work can help make the sub feel sexually objectified in the hottest way and that rush is fun even without any sexual play. On the advanced side, long term and predicament bondage scenes hold particular power.

Tony: Long-term bondage is a pretty intense way to instill control. The first weekend Derek visited me at my home, I had him spend a night locked in a small wooden box at the foot of my bed. He couldn't move much and he could not sit up or lay down in it. The isolation and physical confinement was pretty intense, but it was the heat that led Derek to call the scene. When I unlocked the box, he was in a deep puddle of sweat and was as docile as a newborn kitten.

Derek: Extended bondage has this cycle where at first I try to stay calm and find a comfortable place. But eventually my muscles begin to ache and anger wells up as I struggle to be comfortable or escape. Soon my helplessness becomes a turn on. Eventually, this sexual frustration subsides and I calm down — only to repeat the whole cycle again. Being locked in Tony's box was intense, and being the heavy masochist I am, I was bummed that I couldn't make it through the night without calling for help — but I knew when it was time to ask Tony to check in on me. Self-awareness and clear communication are among the most important skills you can have as a sub.

Bondage can be quite challenging physically, and it can cause harm if care is not taken. It's important not to restrict breathing or blood flow and to avoid nerve impingement. It's up to the sub to communicate such issues but a good top will still check in.

> **Tony:** I have a joke, "Safe words are for retarded tops." Now I don't mean to suggest that safe words don't have their place, but I think the point is clear. Good communication is a key BDSM skill and a major responsibility for tops and bottoms in a scene. "Yellow" is useless, but if you tell me "Sir, my left hand is going numb," then I know how to fix the situation.

Since good communication and monitoring are so important to safety, you can never leave a sub alone in physical bondage. Things can go wrong and without someone around to actively monitor the situation the results can even be fatal.

While it would seem that bondage skills are primarily a top thing, this is far from the truth. The bottom's job is more than just lying there passively — bondage is hard on you and demands a lot of the bottom. So along with good communication skills and body awareness, a really great bondage sub has good core strength, flexibility, and endurance. Learning to regulate breath to extend and focus the scene is an even more advanced skill.

For tops, bondage, and rope bondage in particular, is also its own art and knowing safe rope work is a way of demonstrating skill and creating trust with the sub.

> **Derek:** The first time we met it was only matter of minutes before Tony had my cock and balls out and began tying them up. It was a great introduction. Instantly he showed me his skill, asserted his dominance and made me want more.

Both of us are fond of using rope as a way to seduce boys in bars. There are a lot of guys that are curious about BDSM and seeing the rope often gives a boy an opening to talk about his inner fantasies.

Derek: I love tying up novice boys in bars as a fun way to build trust. He's in public so he knows he's safe — still, it's a big leap of trust. Being made helpless gives him a certain freedom to indulge desires that he may be afraid of. I'm fond of Shibari (Japanese rope bondage) that decorates the boy, makes him feel exposed, objectified and attractive as the center of attention. Even if we never play again, he's taken a first step in exploring an aspect of his sexuality, and that may someday bloom into something that is really rewarding and enjoyable for him.

Tony: Of course, if you're going to seduce a boy, you have to catch his attention first. Sometimes this is as easy as wearing a couple coils of rope on a carabineer attached to your belt. Hell, I've gone as far as standing on a bench in a crowed bar holding a coil above my head, but then I'm subtle like a brick to the face. But, I get the best results attracting the attention of a new boy by running rope on someone I already know, like Derek. This inevitably sparks an interest. Generally, I'll stick to quick binders and fast tie-downs for this purpose... remember most new boys have short attention spans.

As an aside, if you are out and come across a boy in bondage (handcuffs, shackles, restraints, rope, a collar), don't touch unless you get permission. This isn't some abstract Leather/S/m culture etiquette; it's common courtesy. As a top playing in public it can be challenging to control the situation when you have the added element of the public, but it's important that you maintain control and make your boy feel that he is safe and under your control alone.

It's also important to play safely and in public play you should lead by example. Responsible riggers carry safety shears or some other means of safely cutting the rope from their sub and even a flashlight unless they can rely on daylight. They never leave their sub unattended in bondage and they check in frequently. When gags are used, they establish nonverbal signals to indicate distress. They don't tie body parts (like their sub's balls or PA) to stationary objects or fixed points where falling or thrashing could cause injury and they avoid bondage that could cause unintended choking or restriction of breath.

There is a natural progression of learning in rope bondage skills for both the top and the bottom. Most of us start with simple tie-downs and floor work. With these the main goal is learning to do ties that won't tighten up, cutting circulation when the bottom pulls and struggles.

This can progress to more elaborate bondage for sex and play where more aesthetic and functional elements are introduced. Once you get to bondage that needs to support body weight even more skill is required of the top and of the bottom. The most advanced work is rigging for full suspension. It takes a great deal of training and skill for the top to learn to do this safely and it takes a lot of conditioning for a sub to learn to handle full rope suspension for even a fairly short period of time.

Learning the more advanced skills is hard since, as a community, gay men have focused more on areas like whipping and flogging and less on quieter techniques like bondage. So we've both had to go outside the men's community to learn. But this has exposed us to new viewpoints and allowed us to share our community perspectives as well.

Whether partnering for one-on-one training, going to specific bondage workshops or attending major pansexual events like Thunder in the Mountains, there are lots of opportunities to learn if you cannot find teachers in your own community. Of course, as more gay men take on rigging skills, you can expect that we will start to contribute in unique ways as the energy gay men have brought to the BDSM scene is markedly powerful and aggressive.

Derek: I learned my Shibari skills from a straight skinhead friend in the pansexual community. I was lucky in that he was experienced in topping men and as a result he understood how to tie for the male anatomy. We did it as a skills trade and I taught him play piercing techniques in return. For me this one-on-one exchange of skills is the best way to learn new BDSM skills.

Tony: I've been extremely lucky living in the Pacific Northwest where the delineations between the men's, women's, trans and pan communities are not as rigid. I've had some incredible teachers including James Mogul, Max from BondageLessions.com, Twisted Monk and Midori, among others. I'm constantly learning new techniques, stealing ideas and adapting them to my own style.

Rope bondage is a rich and expressive form of control. Because it can enforce power dynamics in so many intense and sensual ways, it is frequently the foundation for our scenes. Even before we met, we both had a deep love of rigging, and when we met that passion for rope allowed us to grow and learn together. In our play, we've created rope rituals that have expanded with our experience and developed new rigging to suit our style of play. We've also learned a lot by teaching others along the way. While the road to rope bondage mastery is long, it is also wide and full of rewards for those that undertake the journey.

THE POWER OF FLUENCY

by LqqkOut

While it sometimes gets me in trouble, I don't often think of the words I use before saying them. More specifically, at some point the complex dance of pronunciation, sentence structure, and grammar become second nature for all of us. Everyone goes through a similar progression when learning to use a new tool. In language we go from babbling to speaking, scribbling to writing, even gesturing to signing — we each endured awkward learning stages to finally master the tremendously powerful tool of communication.

Though more commonly referred to as "toys," we use all sorts of tools in the kink world. Some people enjoy the primal feel of leather or the rigidity of steel, but I identify with the fluidity and complexity of rope. As a tool, rope's form follows its function. With it, you can emulate dozens of other items including cuffs, restraints, floggers, whips, blindfolds, gags, hoists, and harnesses. While I used to say that it was a cheap way to fill a toybag, my obsession and subsequent rope collection rendered that point moot! Still, the benefit of having a tool of such diversity ready for immediate use allows you to take advantage of any situation — versus pausing the scene to dig a flogger out of the toybag or wishing you had smaller cuffs to keep your partner from wriggling away. Like a perfect dance partner, it follows your lead without getting in your way. Once you can utilize the flexibility of a rope, you have tapped into tremendous potential. Of course, the hardest part is getting to that point!

My first experiences with bondage were clumsy. I had no idea what I was doing, but I knew it was fun! I started playing with rope out of sheer curiosity. It was a toy — a daring, boredom-banishing way to spice things up with my partner. In hindsight, I should have seen the slippery slope in front of me — midway through the first tie I needed "just one more piece." I recognize now that it was more than a hot night of fun — it was an important first step in my exploration.

I was hooked. Pretty soon, I replaced my fumbling attempts at bondage with ties found online and in books. My first bondage partner and I eventually separated, and with a sense of detachment I put the ropes away alongside the cheap vibrator, "cherry" flavored lube, naughty dice, and an uncomfortable butt plug — a land of misfit sex toys that I accumulated during my early explorations. Upon seeing my nearly discarded toy box, however, my new lover enthusiastically asked me to tie her up. I dusted off *Jay Wiseman's Erotic Bondage Handbook*, uncoiled the rope, and was back in the game!

At that point, I knew a couple of knots and could tie a basic cuff. I had no idea that my "Authentic Japanese Bondage Rope" with its crimped metal ends and synthetic fibers was anything but authentic or Japanese. It was still a toy — titillating, fun to pull out, use for sex, and then put away for next time. I had little use for it outside of the bedroom. However, as a stubborn geek, I wanted to learn how and why things work so I began studying, attending workshops, and practicing new techniques. I was especially drawn to rope because I was intrigued with its technical aspects and complexity. Since so many people say rope is difficult, I wanted to prove to them and myself that it wasn't *that* bad.

I was wrong! Reading instructions is one thing, but the trial and error while fumbling with new techniques and styles proved much more difficult. Eventually, I exhausted the ties in my how-to books and could get through a scene without the instructions. While many people avoid the time investment, the challenge of continual learning kept me interested in researching, experimenting, and practicing.

I may have become a rope geek, but my favorite part of kinky sex has always been the multitude of toys! If one doesn't fit within a particular scene, ten others can take its place. Over time, I've built a unique collection of personal favorites that resonate with my play style. However, even with the wide variety of available toys, everyone seems to find a specialty. In my case, rope consistently winds its way into scenes, inspired by the work of world-renowned rope artists. I was impressed by their ad-lib approach during performances, demos, and scenes. I realized they were expertly orchestrating not only the ties, but also the emotion, connection, and energy that they shared with their partners. In their hands, the rope is no longer only a tool or toy; instead, it is an extension of their will.

Fortunately members of the rope world are eager to share their knowledge with the community by contributing to discussion groups, producing dazzling performances, or teaching classes. For me, becoming an educator has not only been a great way to meet people; it also forces me to take new perspectives on the material. By taking a step back to think beyond the recipe-style description of a tie, I uncovered their underlying concepts. As I furthered my understanding, I also gained the confidence to relax and focus on my partner. Rather than listening to my inner critic, I began recognizing new reactions from my partner. Instead of the previously jarring mistakes and interruptions, I took comfort in the familiarity of the rope in my hands as our scenes began to flow.

"Would you mind suspending her while I talk about the beauty and artistry of Japanese style bondage?" So began the demo. While I knew my model from professional (and geeky!) online conversations, we had never met in person and this was to be a strictly academic exercise. She stripped to her lingerie and made clear that I wasn't to touch any place that was still clothed. I couldn't stop thinking about how attractive she was. In fact, I barely heard the speaker, focusing instead on my willing victim. I couldn't hide my intrigue. I went through the motions as I was required for the demo, but as soon as I deviated from the otherwise routine path — the moment I cradled her neck in my hand to relieve her muscles — everything changed. The presenter encouraged the audience to think beyond rope as a toy and instead as an artistic tool. Yet for the two of us, everything else faded away and for a moment we were alone in the world. Inside my ropes, I touched her more deeply than either of us realized I could, and it was amazing.

Learning a new language often starts with a few vocabulary words and a technical breakdown of sentence structure. While rope bondage replaces cognates and conjugation with knots and ties, the general progression remains the same. As beginners, our comprehension builds as we learn the language's basic rules. Initially we can hold a conversation with the help of a translation guide, or at the very least ask for help finding the restroom! Then, after enough practice, we put down the book and begin communicating fluently. Over time, you learn that it's okay to break the originally rigid rules of syntax. Rather than focusing on the specific words, fragments of thought begin to flow and even without perfect grammar, you're still met with understanding.

Once you achieve a certain level of fluency, you open the door to very unexpected and wonderful results. Imagine a piece of the perfect time — your very own Platonic Ideal. Of all the scenes I've had, the best ones require a connection. Whether it stems from an emotional attachment of love, a lust-driven mutual attraction, or unexpected inspiration, the resulting rush is unmistakable. When the planets align in these terrific scenes, I notice very little outside of the bubble that forms around my partner and me. These are the kinds of scenes that, when done in public, tend to draw a crowd with an awe-inspiring woo-woo aura. In this space, distractions diminish and the world distills into an intense connection with my partner. Some call this "flow" — the sense of total immersion in a single moment or the ability to act without doing. At first this happened sporadically; one moment I was nervous that a crowd was watching our scene, then in the next our audience faded into the background. Paradoxically, I continued to improve my skill level by paying less attention to the ropes. By relying on instincts and a go-to set of techniques, the interactions between my partner and I intensified and took center stage.

Fluency stems from an ability to see beyond the immediate. While it can be learned, it often becomes intuitive. If you can tear a concept down and figure out why it works, you're on to something important! For rope, the goal isn't to recall and tie the perfect knot for the job; instead, if you understand how to combine wraps, loops, and twists you can create an effective tie and get on with the scene. In fact, this is where I've come up with some of my best improvised techniques. As you become more fluent, your creativity is unlocked by the confidence to tear down and restart without particular attachment to the "right" way to tie. Since rope's form follows its function, the end result mixes organically with your scene. It becomes a conduit between you and your partner that expresses the strength, complexity, and passion of your connection through its beauty.

I know the language by heart, but each dance of native speakers is different.

"Have you been bound before? Do you have any flexibility or circulation issues I should know about? Is there anywhere that you consider inappropriate to touch?" As I automatically begin the familiar motions of negotiating our scene, I also begin a completely different form of communication. I listen to your tone, watch your body language, and start seeking the connection that will turn this "scene" into a personal exchange of feeling and emotion.

Energy starts flowing long before unwrapping the first bundle of rope. I feel you breathe deeply and relax into my embrace as I rub your shoulders, neck, and back. After slowly running my hands through your hair, I firmly grasp a handful and listen for that oh-so-telling sigh! I draw a length of rope across your neck as I consider the possibilities.

You quiver in anticipation as I grab your wrists together with one hand and begin applying the first rope with the other. I deftly complete the cuff then proceed to add more until you're wearing a chest harness. I relish each moment as I further restrain your legs and feet — wrapping you into a gift that I'll have the pleasure of opening later.

Once you're securely bound I stare at you on the floor and catch my breath. As the scene progressed, our slow, soft poetic energy gave way to a giggling, playful struggle and finally to fast and aggressive tying — retaliation for a painfully unexpected bite. I catch your eyes then purposefully break contact — leaving you to wonder and allowing me to remember the steps I took to complete the tie. Even the fluent forget the words they meant to say from time to time.

Most of the rope is second nature, leaving me free to follow the emotions of the scene — gently exploring your body, playfully tickling, and aggressively binding — without consciously switching gears between contexts. Yet sometimes you surprise me, and I find myself wanting to learn the intricacies of your dialect, even when our words are the same.

After savoring you a while longer, I begin untying. Rather than remembering and reversing my earlier steps, I let my hands feel their way through the process. I vary my speed as I continue; at times I pause to pull you close using the remaining wraps and breathe into your ear or kiss your body. Once untied, I wrap you in a blanket, scoop you into my arms, and caress your rope marks. The scene continues after the final rope comes off and we drift away together.

In the end, fluency is merely another step along the path of learning. While it was once just a fun toy or a foreign and ancient tool, rope has become an extension of my will. I no longer feel stressed in the heat of the moment while trying to remember a tie. Instead, I take comfort in the familiar motions as I build an intense connection with my partner, switching seamlessly between rigger, top, dominant, and lover. Ultimately, through this personal journey, each of our paths will lead us toward our own unique play style — a personal dialect in a language shared by all.

BONDAGE AND VULNERABILITY

by Sarah Sloane

Bondage is a one of the most powerful tools in our kinky lexicon for challenging our preconceived notions about ourselves and our relationships with others. This is especially true when it comes to issues of power and surrender. It allows us to more fully explore states of physical and psychological helplessness, and work through the resulting opportunities for expansion of power exchange, creation of cathartic experiences, and exploration of our own perceptions of power and vulnerability. In fact, it does so in a way which is wholly unique — in order to be successful, we must work co-creatively with our partner(s) to plan and carry out a scene that pushes the limits of our physical and emotional boundaries. The bottom, once the bondage is in place, cannot easily escape the scene, and must face head on the resulting feelings and experiences that come up for them; their top, in exchange, must act as protector and guide to the bottom, enabling them to have a safe experiences walking through the fire of their psyche.

Because of all of these things, bondage is a type of scene that immediately challenges the people playing to confront the issue of vulnerability. Vulnerability — strictly defined as being in a position where we are able to be wounded or harmed, and must therefore trust the people around us — is difficult for many people to handle. In fact, it's antithetical to the way Western cultures socialize us to live. We're taught early on that being vulnerable is not desirable — that we should be utterly self reliant, we should always keep our personal power and not "give it away", that we should be able to be constantly strong and constantly in control.

Vulnerability has often confused with weakness of the heart and mind; a person who opens themselves to the potential for harm at the hands of another is seen as codependent or needy. People who are socialized as men have a particularly challenging time with it; it flies in the face of the idea of the man as breadwinner, protector, hunter, and head of the household. Unfortunately, one of the unintended aftereffects of the first surges of the feminist movement is that society doesn't see as much value in a woman who appears weak, or helpless, thus giving them a whole new set of behaviors to feel ashamed about.

On the positive side of the question of vulnerability, bondage can give the players an opportunity to create a "safe space" in which they can experience strong emotion and physical reaction. Their anger and rage can be safely contained. They can arch their body and strain against the ropes or straps in an effort to move away from the sensations they are experiencing. They can even be held securely while potentially dangerous items are held to their skin or moved against their most sensitive spots. Because of the combination of vulnerability and creating a safe space, many people find bondage scenes to be particularly catharsis — inducing, and seek out these scenes specifically as part of the process of doing deeper internal work during BDSM encounters. Catharsis can be as simple as having a good cry or even just feeling cared for and protected. It can also be as intense as painfully hard laughing, forced orgasms, out of body experiences, altered states of consciousness, and raging anger releases.

These cathartic scenes — scenes that invoke a purging of emotion, or an ability to bring psychological issues up to the surface and release them — can be particularly difficult, both to direct and to submit to. A bottom who is experiencing catharsis may, in fact, be unable to use a safe word, and may give off the sense of either being fully in control of the situation (when they aren't) or totally out of control and not okay (when they really are). The top must be able to use their gut instincts as well as their knowledge of the person that they're playing with in order to determine if, when, and how a scene should continue or end.

Cathartic play, at least in my ideal, is not a single scene, but an ongoing way to use BDSM as a touchstone for personal growth. Cathartic play, especially with someone that we have a deep level of trust in, can give us a chance to walk farther down a path of self-knowledge and self-awareness than we could easily walk by ourselves. It lets us experience emotions in the crucible of sadomasochism, test our own assumptions about who we are and how strong we are, and challenge ourselves to become stronger, more responsible, more capable than we were before. We carve out a moment in time when we are free of the daily life responsibilities and we can move through space that we create, with our partners, for the sole purpose of giving us a chance to be one portion of who we are — our animal selves, or our emotional selves, or our spiritual bodies. We cheat death, we are not as simple as what we seem to be, and we come together with another soul to lay it all out on the line. Cathartic scenes let our play transform us, and then pick up our newly-changed selves and move back into the world we live in, hopefully better, stronger, and more authentically ourselves than ever before.

One way that a top can do this is to negotiate specifically about how their partner may look and/or feel during a cathartic scene — asking questions like "when you're really in trouble, what does that look and feel like" or "how might I know the difference between you getting the challenges that you want and you being overwhelmed" are a good place to start. Often, the bottom may not know what to say, particularly if they haven't had a cathartic scene that they were able to "debrief" from and find out what the top saw and felt. In those cases, talking about what might happen and how both people feel about where the scene might go is a great way to explore trust and get ideas for what the direction of the scene might be.

While in the process of negotiating, the top will want to ask questions to encourage the bottom to talk about their experiences of feeling helpless, needy, and alone during scenes as well as in their life in general. Often, a bottom who has a history of abject powerlessness in their histories — dealing with abuse or neglect, abandonment, violence aimed at them — will have significant issues in dealing head-on with being vulnerable, not only in the bondage scene but in their life in general. On the other hand, a bottom who has a history of being the strong person, the leader, the protector, or the go-to person may have similar challenges with allowing themselves to be vulnerable, either because they simply don't know how to do so, or because they fear it. Discovering more about the bottom's concepts of vulnerability, as it relates to their out-of-scene lives, can guide the top into managing the scene in a way that is more positive and productive for everyone involved.

It's also important for the top to recognize their own issues around vulnerability. Many people choose the top role because they are uncomfortable with their own inability to release control; in particular, they may find that guiding a scene in which the bottom is fighting with these same issues gives them a difficult view in the mirror, one that needs to be addressed after the scene is over. It's also challenging for some tops to be on the receiving end of a cathartic explosion from the bottom, particularly one in which the bottom is crying or screaming at the top. Finding a way to communicate emotional limits before and after the scene is key — the top isn't simply an automaton that is not affected by the people they play with, and it's sometimes important to reinforce that idea with the bottom.

Entering into a cathartic scene with intent is key; the direction and information yielded by the negotiation should help to define that, but stating it clearly and having everyone involved "buy in" to the intent creates an environment where the goal of the scene is not blocked by confusion or lack of communication. Knowing where you want to go, understanding how you plan to try to get there, and knowing that it's a mutual decision goes a long way towards giving all the players the peace of mind needed to help the letting go process. Understanding that catharsis can be messy is also important; knowing that everyone is making a commitment to be present during the scene, physically and emotionally, can provide the reassurance needed to create that safe space that is so important in charged scenes.

Keep in mind that, regardless of how much you create intent, the scene will not always go the way that you want it to. We often hit roadblocks that have nothing to do with the players — the room may be too cold or too bright, there may be the wrong kind of ambient noise, or any one of a number of environmental factors may not be right. Additionally, our bodies may not be in the mood to play where our minds are willing to go — we may be unable to handle the bondage that time like we did two weeks before, or we may have a rope that pinches in a way that we can't change and move forward. Having a "no harm, no foul" attitude about cathartic scenes is important — some days, it just doesn't work, and it doesn't pay to try to force the issue. However, some people find that they can change the direction mid-scene — what was planned to be a full body suspension may turn out to be floor work, or the intent to get to catharsis through discomfort may become the desire to laugh it out. Again, the negotiation that happened pre-scene can help the top (and the bottom) to realize when the direction needs to change, communicate that fact in whatever way is necessary, and keep moving forward with the scene rather than ending it and trying again another day.

Once the scene is over, regardless of its success and the glowiness of all of the players, it's time for the aftercare. Aftercare for cathartic scenes is important on a lot of different levels. First of all, it's always important to have some closure after any scene, and the aftercare can provide that. Whether it's both partners cleaning up the play area and coiling rope, or curling up in a corner for some snuggles or heavy-duty making out, a chance to reconnect on a "real world" level can help people to sink back into reality in a way that doesn't feel rushed or pushed. Second, cathartic scenes can often bring up feelings of inadequacy, anger, fear, frustration, or other uncomfortable emotions for all involved. Having a chance to check in with each other a day or so after the scene can get us beyond the feeling of uncertainty in dealing with the other persons involved. It can also give us a chance to see ourselves and our actions and reactions through another person's eyes. What felt like weakness and "giving up" might actually be seen as a yielding to forces that were greater than what one could stand up to, and having that idea re-framed by one's partner can be a self-esteem enhancing moment.

Even tops often have feelings of anger at themselves or insecurity after heavy scenes; often, they want to do the absolute best for their partner and they don't find themselves matching up to their own expectations of themselves. A compassionate, caring bottom can have an amazing impact by simply reaffirming that the top did a great job in the scene. Finally, aftercare that happens in the days and weeks after the play date is important after heavy scenes because often we don't know what might be uncovered, emotionally or physically, until well after the initial aftereffects are gone. Knowing that we can check in with our partner and discuss insights and ask questions, even weeks after the scene is over, can be an amazing opportunity to learn to trust someone even more deeply, and to enable additional healing and growth to happen with the newly-discovered information that arises.

Our experiences as bondage players, over time, help us to not only see the possibility in delving into the deeper parts of our psyches, but also help us to consciously create scenes that offer a moment of growth through catharsis. Being able to experience our vulnerability as something that is not seen as weakness, but rather as strength — being able to come together with our partners and create an opportunity to release negative emotions in a way that is healing — these take us beyond the mundane into the extraordinary. As we live, we grow; as we love, we change. Anything that we can do to bring ourselves to a point of a more healing, more authentic experience of ourselves is an amazing gift. And to be able to do it, cooperatively with another person, is an extraordinary joy.

I WAS ME: ALONE IN A CROWD

by Klawdya Rothschild

I'm upside down, just high enough off the ground for my hair to drag on the floor but not for my head to touch. My left leg is bound tight, bent backwards pointing to my right, and my right leg is strapped with a taut line straight to the top of the rack. The music all around me is fast and throbbing and my heart is pounding in a furious effort to catch up causing my pulse to push against the ropes with every beat. There I am hanging, as I feel the beginnings of a bruise and a smile starting to form. I stretch to reach for my next piece of rope, and use my body weight to swing closer to where I staged it. Just when I grab the rope and pull it into me, it happens:

"Do you want some help with that?"

"No, but thanks." I say straining a smile despite the swollen blood-filled face caused by my inversion suspension.

I often find myself in a public play space of an SM event, after a long day, week, or weekend of working. The stress of social situations, separation from partners, and the rawness that comes from having no alone time and always being "on stage" builds a frantic energy in my limbs that needs to be pumped out. Even though I am exhausted, when I finally get a spare moment I make a B-line for the nearest available suspension frame. I am not here to put on a show; I am here in a race against time to bundle myself up, hard and fast. During this time, inside my ropes, I have escaped to a new dimension, a new plane, I'm off the ground and off the planet simultaneously. I have removed myself; I have seceded from the union. I have penned my Declaration of Independence in rope. Through the gesture of my rope pen, I have claimed myself, *reclaimed* myself from the demands of social expectations. My status reads: "I'm a little tied up at the moment". Needing or wanting to please is gone.

"It can't be as much fun to play by yourself."

I just smile. You just don't understand, I think to myself. Here I am, flying through the air with rope in my hands. I can go anywhere right now, what do I need you for? I laugh. This rope in my hands is my ticket to freedom, and like Wonder Woman, this lasso will reveal truths hidden within the person it encircles— and right now that person is me. I can laugh about it now, the ignorance of someone who can't understand the comfort I find bound within my own ropes, but it took me a long time to get there myself.

The first time I tied myself up I was still under the illusion that I was a cold and sadistic Domina, 100%. I had surrounded myself, my entire life with clients, servants, and eager pupils — that's how I wanted it. My relationships were for function, not for fun, and I didn't understand the difference. It was never important to me to know other skilled tops, let alone riggers, and if I became acquainted with one I probably would have considered that person competition, or even jealous of me. It wasn't until I wrote and started working on a performance where a large group of us would all be suspended and interconnected that I began to realize the need for my fellow performers to also be able to rig. But who would tie me? I realized with a flash of anxiety like a fist to the gut that my ego (my vision of self as top only), was in direct conflict with my artwork (my vision of self within the world). This is when it first hit me:

"I can tie myself up!"

Like any deluded egomaniac, I thought I invented it. I thought surely within the confines of Bondage, let alone D/s, that no one would have sidestepped the otherwise necessary power exchange. No one would have willingly rendered power dynamics insignificant. "Haha, I've foiled you *submission*," I thought to myself, "you'll never get me to break role!" So up I went. I reversed the schematics in my mind, and used myself as my own demo bunny to teach my cast and crew to tie.

I was hooked. Maybe I realized that this was true power. This was absolute control. I didn't need a top before and now I didn't even need a bottom. I had myself, and my rope, and that was all I needed. All bondage is a conversation between tie-er, rope, and tie-ee. The rope works as a tool to hold, transfer, take, and give power as much physically and psychologically as symbolically and conceptually. Self-bondage, unlike bondage with the dichotomy of top and bottom has no one determined power dynamic. The power is a fluid thing because I am simultaneously in control and not in control. Through Self-Bondage as a practice I am defining my limits, in addition to testing and pushing them. Using rope I define the literal limits of my body, and the tighter to tightest they go show me my physical volume, and beyond that my physical endurance.

My suspension rig is an 8 foot steel cube with hard points in every possible direction. I kept it in my studio/dungeon with the rest of my equipment set up for private sessions, rehearsals and photo shoots. After my Self-bondage revelation I moved my suspension rig above my bed. Here I could experiment safely hidden from the rest of the world. In this space, my room, my rig, my rope, the conversation had a singularity enforced by the presence of only one point of view. Alone in my room, I am me from the moment I enter the door. With or without bondage I have only myself to rely upon in the event of anything. In this sense living alone or being alone in your dwelling is a form of self-bondage. It requires all the discipline and control of tending a captive, with only you at the beginning and the end of all intentions.

I went from being a self-serving Domme to cutting the "other" out of the equation. At times this solitude is exactly what I need: the solace of self-service. I can reclaim myself from the entire world. I can seduce myself with rope. Alone I decide to stand or kneel at the onset. I can play music, my music, my favorite music, and set my own mood. I can light candles and dedicate the space and intentions to myself, to my needs, and shamelessly pursue my desires and my outcomes. With Self-bondage I feel the weight and strength of my bodywork on every part of me at once. I can feel every breath I take push against the harness around my chest, and pull that tension through my legs and up into the frame. The ropes guide force, my energy, my tension, my thoughts, my hopes, my dreams all over. The ropes take that force up and out of me into the air, or through me and down to the ground and then back into me. I become a generator of electric impulse and the ropes are my conduit, my messenger. In Self-bondage I am squarely at the center of my universe, not someone-else's and not for anyone else. I have a place and I am in it.

Who has shown me who I am? How did I get there?

I take a moment to smell the sweet grass scent of the raw hemp and let the ropes fall onto my face, and tumble down my bare shoulders before I gather it all together again, fast, so I feel its natural tooth bite me with each successive inch. I want every part of myself alive. I want to take it all in. I want to give this to myself. Alone, self-serving, no one can or will provide you with what you need. No one ever knows better what you want, what you secretly crave; indulgence, here, is unmitigated. In my home, I can make a haven for myself, away from the world around me — and with rope I can fully escape.

In this escape I have a choice. I can escape from myself, avoiding my thoughts or the pressures of daily life and I can use the ropes to strip away conventional rules like gravity, the boundaries of pain and pleasure, the cans and can'ts, the dos or don'ts. In this state of mind I am unburdened by the pressures of the other. The rope also allows me to escape into myself, work out my thoughts and stresses, meditate on my hopes and wishes with the unraveling of rope, the tying and untying of knots. If I cry no one sees my make-up run, if I scream no one screams back. Alone I tackle the contortion of my body within my rope, and I cast my net to pull myself out of the wild churning ocean of the outside world.

It was through this that I realized that I wasn't a Domme, and then I retired. I erased my client lists and unlocked my stable to set my chattel free. I began my journey as a bondage switch and I haven't looked back. There was just one problem: aside from myself there was still no one around who could tie me. So I began, once again, to seek the "other".

Who am I? What am I doing here?

These are the questions I ask myself every time I walk into a room not my own. The room changes, but my questions stay the same. I may not always know what my next step is, but I at least try to figure out what I am walking towards. It is this intentionality that makes me aware of how vulnerable I am. Then I can admit that I walk around in a state of constant exposure, laid bare to everyone around me. To the outside world I may seem closed and hard, lacquered and perfect; without my Domina ego to inflate

I am all too aware that I am susceptible to the thoughts, looks and desires of the others around me. When I am upside-down or immobilized, bruised or burned by rope I am truly vulnerable, but it's a kind of vulnerability that is understood by all. Rigging causes sweat to wipe away off my makeup. Hanging dishevels my clothes, and bruises my skin. I may look around, eager to find someone to play with, but knowing that with my newfound powerlessness I am too afraid to be able to express this longing. The result of this fear is that I feel the most alone when I am in a crowd of people. I crave the bondage because it takes away my shell, and when I do the tying my focus is fully diverted from the fear, fully diverted from the loneliness, and fully diverted from the unfulfillable desire for "other".

I walk into the middle of the room. As I begin to stretch. I open all of the muscles in my body, one by one. I warm up to my environment and I attempt to block out the vibrations of the noise and the light shining in people's eyes as they watch me. They wonder what I am going to do. Some wonder who I am waiting for, who I will string up or who will play with me. I smile to myself and wonder the same thing. At this point in my scene I do not know and I do not want to know where I am going to take myself. The only way I can stand to be alone in a crowd is to shut my mind off. Thought has no place is this meditation, this journey of intuition. I need to show what I am capable of, and I need to show this to them as much as I need to show it to myself. I will always have myself and the rope slung over my back. As much as I may want someone else to play with, once I open my bag and the first rope unfurls I am in scene, committed to that moment, and committed to myself.

The best way I have found to take myself on a blind journey is to pre-set one anchor point, and several lengths of rope on the rig itself. Once I anchor myself I can fly, and I have addressed my need for safety enough to go anywhere from there. One by one I add more rope, changing positions, decreasing mobility, until there is no more left. Both of my hands are tied, my legs, my trunk, even my hair, my toes, and my nipples. There I hang, suspended, caught on view for all to see. I begin to writhe in the ropes, to struggle against them until I exhaust myself, and just dangle. The ropes hold me for me; they hold me for a proverbial "you" or "you all". The rope wraps me as though in the arms of a partner, comforting me, reassuring me that I cannot go anywhere. In that moment I belong to the rope, to myself, and to all who watch me. Whether you realize it or not, without your involvement and before your very eyes I have given away control, by taking power over myself completely. I have gotten you to play with me the only way

I know how. I have pulled you in to my exchange. As my passive partners, my onlookers, you stand and watch as the unwitting foil playing with me in my power saga.

BIOGRAPHIES

Ariana Dawnhawk and Ryan

Ryan's background with witchcraft began in the Reclaiming Tradition, and Ari started out in NeoWicca; both of these are still parts of their respective paths. They apprenticed for two years with an initiate of the Anderson Feri Tradition, and are seeking further training. They both are Thelemites, part of a religion, magical system, and philosophy that emphasizes will development, which gained popularity with Aleister Crowley. They are also initiates in Crowley's Ordo Templi Orientis, and much of their practice in ceremonial magick comes from the O.T.O. Their other spiritual influences include Neos Alexandria, a group of Greco-Roman-Egyptian syncretists, and the Department, a small group of people teaching, mentoring, and learning with each other.

Ari and Ryan have been exploring kink almost as long as they have been together. This began with rope bondage and has branched out into other aspects of BDSM. They are actively involved in their local kink community.

Coral Mallow

Coral is a force of nature, and because of that the most interesting things occur in her general vicinity. In an effort to be more than just the Universe's cat toy, she has pooled her energies into enjoying life, from chocolate to flesh hooks, boys to girls, books to super powers, and boots to gloves! Always in pursuit of knowledge and a good story, she can be found talking to just about anyone. Coral is proud to have served her community as Ms. Oregon Leather 2007. She is an educator, artist, Ordeal Path Worker, body pride advocate, model, gamer/comic geek, mentor, and honored to be the Owner of her property, Ryan. She can be contacted at hooksandchocolate@yahoo.com.

Esinem/Bruce Argue

Bruce Argue, better known as Esinem, is a well-know figure on the bondage scene, whose work features in wide range of publications, including SM Sniper, Time Out, Forum, Bizarre, Metro, web sites and video/photography (one and off-camera). Recent projects have been taking bondage into mainstream: Binding a model for one of Jamie McCartney's body castings; opening the Agent Provocateur new season's launch party; a shoot with Manuel Vason for the art magazine ".Cent" and preparing bound tailor's dummies for "Patlab's installation in Zurich", "The Lost Spaces of Stiller". He performs internationally at events such as Torture Garden, Rubber Ball, Nuit Demonia, Wasteland and The Clinic, runs one of the largest free Japanese style bondage web sites (www.esinem.com) and teaches regular bondage classes in London (www.esinem.com/main-tuition). Whilst his style is influenced by kinbaku, having studied with Arisue Go and more recently with Osada Steve, his performances range from serene and traditional to political and shocking. Audience comments almost invariably mention the obvious chemistry between him and his partner and main model, Electric Fairie.

Graydancer

Graydancer, Ninja Sex Poodle and Ronin of Love, comes from the venerable rope bondage tradition of Madison, WI, where he honed his craft to become the world premiere podcaster of rope bondage with "the Ropecast". He has presented and performed at venues across North America and is the creator of the GRUE (Graydancer's Ropetastic Unconference Extravaganza), a grass-roots kink event held in various cities. His writing has been published in Secret, Power Exchange Magazine, and several anthologies. He is also the author of three self-published novels of erotic magic: Nawashi, Jujun, and the forthcoming Kumir, available in print, audio, and e-book formats. Currently Graydancer plies his trade as an itinerant rope top, burlesque performer and kink educator, smiting the evil of sloppy ends wherever they may lie. His work can be found at www.graydancer.com and www.ropecast.net.

Janice Stine

Janice Stine is many things to many people: Ms. J, Mistress Mary Poppins, A toaster, a chew toy... The list goes on. If you try to put her in a box, she'll deconstruct it, color it with glitter pens, and turn it into something unexpected. Kink just happens to be an outlet where her creativity and love of the absurd can be channeled. For Janice, the conventions of the scene are not hard and fast rules, but rather tools that she can mold and use to create something that is all her own. She identifies less as an educator and more as an avid learner, who will happily share whatever skills and lessons she acquires on her journey, so that others may carve out their own path. In her experience, BDSM is all about individuals enjoying and taking charge of their own sexual preference, not trying to fit themselves into predefined roles.

JD of Two Knotty Boys

JD is best known for his work as one of the Two Knotty Boys, the rope bondage instruction team that gained international acclaim for their popular guidebooks, "Two Knotty Boys Showing You the Ropes" (2006) and "Two Knotty Boys Back on the Ropes" (2009). A consummate educator, JD is also the producer of over 100 rope bondage video tutorials, posting an average of one tutorial, online, every week, for two years. With an easygoing, lighthearted and compassion focused teaching style, JD continues to expand the possibilities of what can be achieved through rope bondage. His collaborative workshops, books and videos have informed and inspired thousands of individuals, and his writings provide a rare insight into the philosophy behind his work. For more information visit www.twoknottyboys.com.

Klawdya Rothschild

Klawdya Rothschild is an independent curator, artist, Alternative Sexuality and Spirituality educator, Kink Rights Advocate, and Occultist. Klawdya's academic background is in Social and Evolutionary Psychology, Fiber Arts, and Curating. In 2008 she was elected to the Board of Directors of the National Coalition for Sexual Freedom (NCSF) and has participated in the BDSM/Fetish communities for over a decade. She has worked as a professional Dominatrix, a model and performer, Rope Bondage Rigger, a Spiritual Healer, a Temple Whore and always a mixed-media artist. As founder of the Property Project (www.PropertyProject.org), an international artist community, she created the Synchronetic Tarot, documenting sex, magick and fetish in ecstatic, public and private rituals. In the BDSM and Fetish Community she is well known for Japanese-influenced Rope Bondage, especially her Self Bondage Manifesto, and for CDTV Transformation and Sissification. She is the founder of the Baltimore Erotic Arts Festival, and a recipient of the Annie Sprinkle Aphrodite Award for Sexual Service to the Community. Klawdya hopes to broaden the scope of alternative practices by educating non-alternative communities and to foster a sense of community within and between alternative groups.

LadyGold

In spite of her scene name, LadyGold is a submissive and has been all of her kinky life. She was given the name by a former Owner some 12 years ago and as she says, "It would seem silly to refer to herself as "the submissive formerly known as "LadyGold" even though the relationship no longer exists. Although she has never competed for any Leather titles, she has presented workshops all over the country and is very proud to have been invited back to teach at Shibaricon for six consecutive years.

Lee Harrington

Lee Harrington is an eclectic artist, spiritual and erotic educator, gender radical and published author and editor on human sexuality and spiritual experience – including "Shibari You Can Use: Japanese Rope Bondage and Erotic Macramé" and the "Toybag Guide to Age Play". Well known for his fun and informative approach to education, he approaches sexuality as yet another art to master, or simply an art to enjoy to its fullest! He has been an active part of the international kink and sex positive communities for over 13 years, and his stories make people laugh while showing you that eroticism can be as serious, sexy, or silly as you make it. Lee's writings and photography have appeared in numerous anthologies including "Dark Moon Rising: Pagan BDSM and the Ordeal Path" (also under his previous pen name, Bridgett Harrington), and his image has been seen everywhere from PlayBoy TV to the pages of Skin Two Magazine. To learn more about Lee visit www.PassionAndSoul.com.

Lochai (cover art)

Lochai is an award winning photographer, renowned bondage rigger, educator, and stalwart of the greater BDSM CommUNITY who has been teaching in the public kink scene for thirteen years. In 2008 he was picked to spearhead the internationally renown Hogtied.com adult site, while still teaching erotic rope, performing, and monitoring and organizing online communication platforms such as the

AlternativePresenters.com, which he created. By bringing an eye for beauty, passion for his craft, and playful irreverence to all of his endeavors, Lochai's work stands out, and yet he freely shares his skills and knowledge to rope enthusiasts and photographers of all experience levels and from all walks of life.

His photography has been judged "The World's Most Erotic Photograph" by Erotic Signature, stands in the permanent collection of The Leather Archives in Chicago as well as in the World Erotic Art Museum in Miami. In addition it has been published in such publications as British Journal of Photography, World's Greatest Erotic Art of Today Vol. I and II, Secret, Skin Two, Bizarre, Prometheus, Cherry, A Magazine, Fetish Anthology, and

Extreme Anthology as well as his own fine art photography books. To learn more about Lochai visit Kirinawa.com.

LqqkOut

LqqkOut is a fun-loving rope geek and sex educator who has found a home in the Midwest kink community. When he's not traveling to events, he contributes to the Iowa State University CUFFS student group and serves on he board of Minneapolis TNG group Min-KY. Although he's a relatively new member of the scene, LqqkOut has presented at numerous events across the country, including Kinky Kollege, Shibaricon, Denver Bound, and Beyond Leather. LqqkOut is continually developing his rope style and owes his knowledge and success to many of the world's foremost riggers, including Lochai, JimiTatu, and the rest of the Shibaricon crew, Osada Steve (Tokyo), Mark from DV8 House (Sydney), and Zamil (Berlin). As an educator, LqqkOut aims to provide a comfortable down-to-earth learning environment for all genders, orientations, and experience levels. You can find his long list of presentations, events, and class materials at his website www.kinkfriendly.org

Madison Young

Madison Young is a San Francisco based writer, artist, director, and adult performer. She engages in panels and facilitates workshops around the country on bdsm, feminism, art and pornography. She is the artistic director of the award winning sex positive queer art gallery and performance space, Femina Potens. Madison's writings have appeared in such publications as On Our Backs, Girlfriends Magazine, and the anthology "Baby Remember My Name". Madison has been featured on MTV"s LOGO channel program "Out and About", the documentary Lesbian Sex and Sexuality Porn Today; Pushing the Limits, IFC's program "Deeper with Dave Navarro" and was featured in Brian Alexander's recent book release "America Unzipped". Madison has won numerous awards for her work in the adult industry including the Feminist Porn Award, Best SM Suspension Model from Bishop Awards and voted one of the top ten bondage models by BondageAwards.com. Her forthcoming book "The Tail of a Bondage Model" is expected to be released in late 2009. For more information visit www.FeminaPotens.org and www.MadisonBound.com.

Maria Shadoes

Smart Assed Switch (SAS), sexual leaning bottom and creative leaning Top, Maria Shadoes taught, traveled and performed for over five years with Lew Rubens around the United States, Caribbean and Europe. In that time she modeled for hundreds of internet sites and movies gaining invaluable experience on both sides of the rope. She is now known in her own right as a model, bondage instructor (in the western style, from rope handling to suspension and predicament ties) and inventor of the "Endless Bondage" school of rope work. In the coming years keep an eye out for her how-to videos, continued work in bondage videos and websites (including her own www. BoundToLoveIt.com), and more!

Mark Yu

Mark Yu is a Kinbaku/Nawa Shibari practitioner and educator. He is a devotee of Chinese medicine, Taoist sexual yoga and Zen. He has developed and advocates a style of progressive rope-based body disciplines that has the power to transform and heal, as well as look good and satisfy. He has taught bondage, healing arts and energetic play techniques publicly and privately for several years. Drawing from his lifetime study of Oriental Medicine, 25 years of clinical experience in treating muscle pain and bio-mechanical dysfunction and his extensive knowledge of the body and its energy pathways, he has designed a beautiful and practical approach to the increasingly popular and wonderfully erotic techniques of rope restraint and body manipulation. He is director and curator of The Jade Gate, a center for Erotic Art and Culture in Austin, Texas. He is the owner of The Jade Gate web log, http://jadegate.blogspot.com.

Sarah Sloane

Sarah Sloane is a queer polyamorous sadomasochist from the Washington DC metro area. She is a BDSM / Polyamory / Sexuality educator who has taught literally hundreds of classes for kink, leather, fetish, and general sex education to for-profit and not-for-profit shops, events, and organizations around the world. She also works with individuals to learn skills and techniques to enhance their lives. She works as a writer and sex educator, a personal / virtual assistant, is the Contributing Editor for Tristan Taormino's Double T Newsletter, acts as a "sexpert" for various sex positive websites, and is available for life coaching and mentoring sessions both in person and via phone. You can find her writing on her website, www.sarahsloane.net.

Tonbi

Tonbi has been an active member of the BDSM scene in Sydney, Australia for over 10 years. During that time he has developed a strong passion for rope bondage, and in the past 4 years has begun to share his passion by teaching rope bondage workshops and skill shares through Sydney Leather Pride Association and private group gatherings. He has also had the opportunity to perform at Hellfire Sydney.

Tony Buff and Derek da Silva

As a 24/7 Sir/boy couple Tony Buff and Derek da Silva deliver a unique perspective into the connection and exchange between two of the heaviest and most experienced players in the gay male community. Through activism, demos, workshops, award winning adult videos, a column in Instigator

magazine and impromptu play at BDSM events across the country, Tony and Derek present an approach to truly twisted, safer play built on a foundation of risk mitigation and mutual trust. Tony's website is TonyBuff.com and Derek's is DerekDaSilva.com.

Van Darkholme

Van Darkholme is an established bondage video director and star. Since 2001 Darkholme has operated Muscle Bound Productions, releasing about a dozen films featuring muscular studs in bondage. Darkholme is a devoted practitioner of Shibari, an elaborate and artful form of rope bondage that originated in Japan.

Darkholme is also widely known as an erotic fine art photographer. Bruno Gmünder recently published Darkholme's book of bondage nudes, Male Bondage. In 2008, Darkholme signed with leading fetish erotica studio Kink.com to create a site for the gay market. The site, BoundGods.com, is produced in Kink.com's San Francisco Armory facilities and features many of Darkholme's favorite fetishes, including muscle worship, bondage, SM, and hardcore sex.

Zamil

Zamil, born and raised in Berlin, has been performing on stage since before he turned twenty and has always enjoyed the lights of the stage. Becoming active in the lifestyle in 1999, he began doing BDSM shows in 2003 and became the founder of ArtSensual project (ArtSensual.com) with his partner maliZ. ArtSensual has become world renown as an established name for high class bondage performances, and has had their work shown in fetish magazines, the daily press and radio stations as well as TV, magazines and podcasts. They have been voted "Best Performer" in 2008 by the international audience at BoundCon.

A teacher by heart, Zamil has spent years as an educator at the college level. In 2004 he traveled to Japan to study traditional Kinbaku techniques at its source, and his patience, focus and fun delivering those traditions and new styles of rope art from Japan has become well known. His newest project with his partners, StudioSIX Berlin (StudioSIX-Berlin.com) was founded to deliver codified Kinbaku techniques directly from Japan to interested students of traditional and contemporary Japanese rope art.

Master/slave Relations

SOLUTIONS 402

LIVING IN HARMONY

Robert J. Rubel, PhD

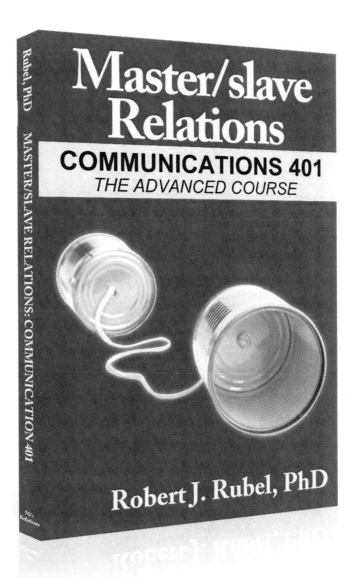

Master/slave Relations

COMMUNICATIONS 401
THE ADVANCED COURSE

Robert J. Rubel, PhD

Master/slave Relations:
Handbook of Theory and Practice

Robert J. Rubel, PhD
Foreword by Jay Wiseman, JD

Rubel

Master/slave Relations

M/s Studies

PROTOCOLS
Handbook for the female slave

Robert J. Rubel, PhD

Protocol Handbook for the Leather Slave: *Theory and Practice*

Robert J. Rubel, PhD

An M/s
Studies
Book

Rubel

PROTOCOL HANDBOOK for the Leather Slave

Squirms, Screams and Squirts

Handbook for Turning Great Sex into Extraordinary Sex

Robert J. Rubel, PhD
Foreword by Jay Wiseman

Power Exchange Books'
Resource Series

AGE
PLAY

Series Editor, Dr. Bob (Bob Rubel)
Issue Coordinators, Sir Colin and his girl, slave kimmie

Power Exchange
Books
art of slavery

Robert J. Rubel, PhD, Series Editor
slave lara, Issue Coordinator

Power Exchange
Books
Playing with Disabilities

Robert J. Rubel, PhD, Series Editor
Angela Stassinopoulos, Issue Coordinator

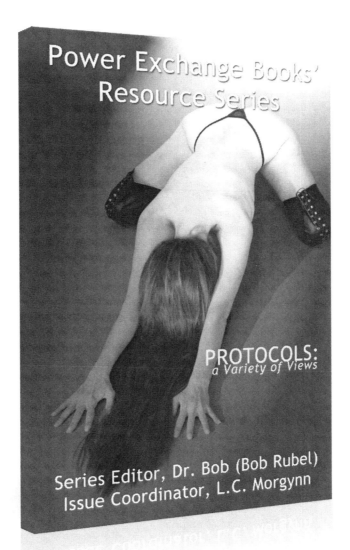

Power Exchange Books'
Resource Series

PROTOCOLS:
a Variety of Views

Series Editor, Dr. Bob (Bob Rubel)
Issue Coordinator, L.C. Morgynn

Titles in Search of Authors

If you are interested in contributing to any of these issues, please contact me at:
PowerExchangeEditor@Yahoo.com

Please say: "Interested in Writing" in the subject line.

- About Power

- Aging M/s Couple, The

- After your Title Year

- Book for submissives, The

- Birth and Training of a Leather Master, The

- BDSM and People of Color

- Book for submissives, The

- Bringing in the Next Generation

- Cigar Play

- Coming Out Kinky: The Joys and Sorrows

- Dressed to Kill: fetish dressing in the world of BDSM

- Exploitation vs Ownership in the M/s Relationship

- Family, Kids, and Kink — Some Challengers

- Finding your Path

- From the Internet to Real Time

- Generational Differences Affecting BDSMers

- Giving Back

- Gorean Relationships

- How to Collect Men

- In Search of Master

- Leadership

- Leather, What is...

- Long-term M/s Relationships -- what keeps them together

- Mentoring — Giving and Receiving

- Multiple Service Relationships

- Objectification

- Physiology – Understanding how the Human Body Responds to SM play

- Prose -- a Collection of Kinky Works

- Symbols, The Importance of

- Shaping Your Power

- Tats, Body Modification, and Scarification

- Transgendered/transsexual

- Vampirism

- What Makes a Master?

CPSIA information can be obtained at www.ICGtesting.com
Printed in the USA
LVOW131835061111

253731LV00012B/207/P

9 781935 509028